Kaizen

Make Process Improvement Fun and Exciting

(How to Create a Lasting Change One Step at a Time)

Elva Curry

Published By **Simon Dough**

Elva Curry

All Rights Reserved

Kaizen: Make Process Improvement Fun and Exciting (How to Create a Lasting Change One Step at a Time)

ISBN 978-1-77485-676-5

No part of this guidebook shall be reproduced in any form without permission in writing from the publisher except in the case of brief quotations embodied in critical articles or reviews.

Legal & Disclaimer

The information contained in this ebook is not designed to replace or take the place of any form of medicine or professional medical advice. The information in this ebook has been provided for educational & entertainment purposes only.

The information contained in this book has been compiled from sources deemed reliable, and it is accurate to the best of the Author's knowledge; however, the Author cannot guarantee its accuracy and validity and cannot be held liable for any errors or omissions. Changes are periodically made to this book. You must consult your doctor or get professional medical advice before using any of the suggested remedies, techniques, or information in this book.

Upon using the information contained in this book, you agree to hold harmless the Author from and against any damages, costs, and expenses, including any legal fees potentially resulting from the application of any of the information provided by this guide. This disclaimer applies to any damages or injury caused by the use and application, whether directly or indirectly, of any advice or information presented, whether for breach of contract, tort, negligence, personal injury, criminal intent, or under any other cause of action.

You agree to accept all risks of using the information presented inside this book. You need to consult a professional medical practitioner in order to ensure you are both able and healthy enough to participate in this program.

TABLE OF CONTENTS

Introduction 1

Chapter 1: Understanding Kaizen 2

Chapter 2: The Kaizen In The Form Of Kaizen Kaizen 7

Chapter 3: Building An Kaizen Culture At Home 13

Chapter 4: Kaizen Methods 18

Chapter 5: A Personal Kaizen 21

Chapter 6: Reach Your Goals With Kaizen 27

Chapter 7: The Basics Of Kaizen Kaizen .. 30

Chapter 8: Kaizen And Business 61

Chapter 9: Kaizen's Benefits 89

Chapter 10: Kaizen And Startups 113

Chapter 11: Ikigai 133

Chapter 12: Additional Uses Of Kaizen . 154

Conclusion 182

Introduction

This book is for those who are looking to improve their lives, or who are hungry or have an inner feeling that there's better way to live. This book is designed for action-oriented people or those who are eager to study.

In this book, you'll be introduced to a fresh method of living your life. A more efficient method. A more simple method. The way to ensure the best results and greater satisfaction within your own life.

The Kaizen method is a potent system of beliefs or principles to live your life according to which can trigger Massive Change and transform your life to improve it.

This book introduces you to the idea of Kaizen and then delves into the ways you can incorporate Personal Kaizen into your life as well as the lives of your family members for the best future.

This is an easy-to-follow guide. It's straightforward information that inspires change and transforms lives

Thank you for purchasing this book. I hope you like it!

Chapter 1: Understanding Kaizen

"Kaizen," as a concept, is used in the context of "Kaizen" is frequently used to describe business procedures that are "continuously developing." You might have guessed, Kaizen is a Japanese concept that was developed by large firms such as Toyota who wanted to teach their employees' mentality the importance of continuously making improvements and changing to best.

More than just a matter to improve personal growth, many executives want to model the way Toyota was able to remain globally competitive despite the fierce competition from the European as well as American counterparts, employed Kaizen.

Writer Matthew May said that Kaizen is an all-in-one idea since it's an exercise, a technique as well as an idea. Many organizations employ the concept to motivate their employees to achieve excellence to increase productivity and the goal of innovation. It is more than a tool; it's an approach therefore, you can benefit from the success of other organizations and implement Kaizen as a method to your personal life.

Change to the Good

The term "Kaizen" is a translation to its Japanese roots in a variety of different ways, but the most common translation is "change to improve."

When you split Kaizen into two distinct vowels, you'll get "Kai" which is a reference to "change," and "zen" which is "good."

When grouped when they are paired, the syllables make an expression that suggests making important improvements that follow the ethos that is embraced by all within the company. The organization encourages every employee to contribute ideas that not only enhance the business but also inspire everyone who is part of the organization.

Effective Kaizen strategy is linked to accountability and the purpose. That is it should yield tangible outcomes that align with the company's goals. For example, Toyota underwent several design modifications before coming up with the perfect hybrid design it released on the market. The decisions made by Toyota ensured that their plan to stay global competitive was fulfilled.

This method can be applied to your personal life. If you have a dream to become a doctor who is successful all that you do should be aligned with your goals. Every single change you make to your lifestyle should bring you an inch or two closer to fulfilling your goal.

Effective Improvements
Kaizen is not about making steps that lead to specific results, without any having any significance. Each time you see your reflection you must ask yourself the following questions:
What's my vision?
What steps should I take to reach this goal?
What changes or sacrifices are I willing to take to help me achieve this vision?
What is the significance of this vision for me?
What is my purpose to accomplish this vision?
Each question needs clear and concrete answers. Without a clear vision, a life is a life that lacks direction.

Imagine having to figure out the escape from a pitch-black room. If you don't turn on the lighting, you are more likely to crash into fixtures, and consequently risk hurting yourself. It's never a good idea to encounter obstacles, but had the lights were on, you could have found the most efficient route out of obstacles quickly.

Vision can bring light to your life. It can alert you to the various obstacles that may occur. It also reduces the chance of suffering injuries.

The third and second questions will require you to have plans, or in addition to the previous metaphor or the blueprint. Blueprints usually contain electronic plans. They'll tell you where the switch is particularly when it is in plain view. It also provides an overview of the hurdles you must overcome before you can reach your goal.

The fourth and final question is to examine your motives. Vision without a purpose is similar to the lightbulb with no electricity. It is what keeps the flame burning. A sense of reason is crucial, particularly at moments when you are facing an obstacle or the sheer number of obstacles that are thrown your path can discourage you.

A lack of vision alone may not stop you from moving forward. Your motivation and determination will be based on your conviction. Your motivation stems from the core of your soul.

The purpose defines the stakes you must meet to achieve your goals. Understanding your mission is the first step to making significant changes to your life.

Chapter 2: The Kaizen In The Form Of Kaizen Kaizen

In the context of corporate software, Kaizen is useful in the context of implementing small modifications to existing business procedures. The changes can be made in size, length, and complexity of projects.

In the words of Toyota, Kaizen has three distinct levels to which different companies can easily modify. The three levels are based on an approach called the Plan-Do-Study-Act (PDSA) technique of solving problems. These will be discussed in the following chapters.

At first, you might think that the language used in this chapter to be too "corporate" due to its many business-related applications, however, as you progress you'll learn and learn how to use all three stages of Kaizen to improve your life.

Three levels of Kaizen
There exist three (3) different levels to Kaizen that are embraced by a variety of well-known organizations around the globe. They are:
1. Large-scale Projects

The majority of organizations focus on small amounts of major projects, primarily because of the lack of resources, budgetary limitations and a limited amount of manpower. Furthermore the risk associated with large-scale improvement projects is more in comparison to smaller improvement projects. The kaizen stage is typically carried out as a result of the necessity.

For example, McDonald's had to cut its ties to Heinz tomato ketchup due to the fact that the company's CEO is the chief executive of McDonald's fierce competitor, Burger King. With McDonald's best interests at heart McDonald's had cut ties with a business associate. This Kaizen degree is commonly called "system Kaizen" or "management Kaizen" by Toyota. It is a systematic process that could either save or destroy the organization.

In real-life applications big projects are similar to taking a vow to your significant other, or to things like a healthier lifestyle. Changes should align with your goal. It is vital to do this while keeping the end in your mind.

Large-scale projects are typically designed. They go through various levels of scrutiny prior to the actual implementation. For example, if you decide to leave your parents' home to become an independent person and live on your own, you don't just go out and leave without planning everything. It is essential to plan all of your plans, including where you'll be staying as well as how you'll be able to meet the challenges of living independently.

2. Mid-Sized Projects

The organizations are separated into various departments according to their roles. There are problems that arise within the department which may not be directly affecting the entire company. For example, its members may decide on issues relating to smaller projects or concerns like purchasing computer systems that are used by IT department. IT department.

There are however companies in which decisions such as these require the approval of the CEO or president. Unfortunately, this is not in line with the Kaizen method. Kaizen advocates the power of subordinates and department head to make their own decisions within their department.

This strategy addresses the decision-making possibilities for all members of the company by using various tried-and-tested strategies such as GE "work-outs" or Six Sigma projects.

Certain, you've taken a number of important decisions throughout your life, such as whether you want to attend college or not , or which course you'll be taking. These are all examples of "large projects." After you've decided on the path you'd like to follow choosing which college offers the most suitable program for the course you want to take counts as an "mid-sized task." The main factors you might want to think about include the proximity to your home or school, fees for students and the campus culture.

Like "large projects" It is crucial to connect "mid-sized initiatives" to your vision and your purpose.

3. Smaller, but Daily Improvements

If there isn't a one drop of water in the ocean, it will never have an ocean. It's the same regarding the Kaizen level. Mid-sized and large-sized projects will fail if those who are involved cannot implement small, daily improvement. For instance, if business leaders are trying to establish an atmosphere that encourages confidence in the employees, then they should be able to give compliments when they are needed. A joking remark could go a long way.

If your goal is to live a healthier life style that not only looks great, but also to be free of health problems Then you should begin by assessing the amount of physical exercise that you engage in on a daily basis. Healthy eating isn't just an occasional thing, it should be a routine.

Another great example is the decision to stop smoking cigarettes. For many, this is an "large undertaking" but the process of stopping smoking completely requires making the effort daily to avoid having to smoke. Smokers may also make incremental adjustments, such as slowly reducing the number of cigarettes they smoke daily.

These small, everyday enhancements are your pennies to the dollar. You should make it count.

Chapter 3: Building An Kaizen Culture At Home

A large portion of your day is spent in your home in the comforts of your own home. It is where you can relax, let your worries go and enjoy yourself. The house gives you a an ambiance of security.

Every house has its own cultural background. They are governed by a tradition and beliefs which may not be the same as the majority of the population. For example, one house may have a tradition of embracing one another, while other homes may be a place of independence.

No matter what the current family culture It is possible to use an Kaizen approach to change the atmosphere of your home to create the kind of environment that promotes productivity among your family members.

Participating Everyone

In a formal organizational setting, the creation of an organizational Kaizen culture demands the involvement of all employees. The resistance to the culture should be dealt with as quickly as possible. Some people are too comfortable with their current system that adjusting to a different system could prove difficult.

Organization leaders tell their members that changing is essential to develop character. It's true, however what all members must be aware of is that the world is changing, The only method to stay relevant is to keep pace or, if you can set the speed at which things are changing.

Culture is the most significant aspect of what makes a human social being. Human beings aren't truly self-sufficient but what they can do is be is interdependent with one another. The bonds that hold an organization or group of people together underlines the importance of the culture.

In a typical family the process of establishing the Kaizen lifestyle can be easy or more challenging based on the degree to which each member is open to changes. The decision-making process at the household is dependent on the cooperation of elders in the family typically the parents, but there are also decisions that family members must make on their own. Kaizen is a firm advocate for families to create a shared vision, which is usually the primary values that all members is able to identify with. Each decision taken by a person to live their life must align with the shared vision of the members of the family.

While the process of evaluating the performance of each individual as a member of the household is not as formal as organisations or companies, maintaining continuous communication and dialog can make what is the distinction between house and an apartment.

Three Steps of Kaizen Culture

It is important not to confuse this with the different levels of Kaizen. There are three (3) phases of Kaizen culture illustrate how change takes place in the family:

First Step: The process to create an Kaizen culture isn't something you can do in a day. Everyone needs to learn to adapt and implement small changes to make bigger improvements. The family's heads must be able to lead the household. They must encourage each family member to think about the purpose they have as family members or members in the family.

The ability to be open to new ideas is essential to inspire enthusiasm and increase an interest in Kaizen. The evaluation of the notion of "self" in a single instance and as members of the family is the first priority.

(This phase typically takes three to six months.)

Second Stage: After the primary purpose of the family is established and the leadership team should be conscious of their efforts to inform each member. Even though the family isn't a formal place making decisions and problem-solving skills will encourage members to take initiative and offer feasible solutions to any challenges that may arise.

The idea of a family that functions as"a "team" and"family "family" is something that should be felt by every family member. (This phase can take (This time can range from six months to a full year)

The Third Stage is where you determine whether the previous two stages are effective. Any decision or change that is made during this stage will naturally align with the ideals and goals of the family. It's as if Kaizen is an established habit for everyone. If at this point, the participants still did not follow the Kaizen method and there was no improvement, then there is a need to re-evaluate the process. Sometimes, the absence of communication among members leads to failure. (Ideally this stage will continue for the rest of your life.)

Cultural Transformation

The primary goal of the Kaizen approach is to review your actions and decision-making process continuously. For an organisation, as instance leaders and employees must continuously search to find "magis."

Magis refers to the Latin word which means "more." The process of making significant changes to your organization or yourself is seeking to satisfy the desire for magis continually. Do not rest on your laurels. changes you as a part of a society that is constantly seeking to make changes.

This transformation in culture can motivate all to take action not just for the group they work for, but for their own lives and the way people live.

Chapter 4: Kaizen Methods

Kaizen is a technique that is best taught through practice. In reality, incorporating Kaizen in your daily life must be a pledge. It isn't a quick fix to all of your issues. It is a daily reminder that you're making improvements that benefit you and those around you. It's as simple as checking whether your actions are in line with your ideals. If your answer is the negative side, then you need to make the necessary changes to ensure that you are on the right path.

"The Five Steps of Kaizen

The first three chapters offered readers an understanding of Kaizen. The next chapter will teach you the five fundamental steps to adding Kaizen to your life

1. Assess

Review your past life. From where you arenow, take the time to recall the most important moments you've reached up to this point. Remember the numerous choices you've made at various crossroads in your life. Examine whether these decisions have helped you or not. Look for potential opportunities which you could improve upon to improve your prospects for the future. Define the various issues you are facing, whether it is financial, emotional, or something other than that.

2. Discussion

Depending on how open you are about your personal life and difficulties, you need to be able to communicate and express how you are feeling and how you need to do regarding it. Talking about your issues does not necessarily mean you have to inform your acquaintances about your problems. Although it can be helpful but introspection can be an excellent thing. It helps to keep the issue and potential solutions in mind. In the end, it's your choice to make it, not theirs.

3. Execute

After you've decided on a course of action, stick to the decision. No matter what the outcome is it is important that your choices and actions align with your fundamental values and goals. If your goals are achieved but at the very least, you have gained something from the experience.

4. Document

Successful organizations that have adopted the Kaizen philosophy, they issue what they refer to"the" Kaizen report. It determines whether the choices or actions have been successful in achieving the objective. It also identifies the various opportunities that have to be considered in the future strategy.

Documentation is crucial for transparency and accountability. Even if you're not part of a company and just want to adhere to the Kaizen method There are ways you can assess and record your decisions so far. (This is discussed in more detail during the subsequent chapter, Your personal Kaizen.)

5. Share

The best part of this age is the fact that you have many ways to talk about and discuss your experiences through your lifetime. Social media such as Facebook, Twitter and LinkedIn allows individuals to discuss and exchange experiences and experiences with others.

This way, you'll be able to learn the opinions of your colleagues and then decide for yourself whether the changes you've made have been successful or if there are additional possibilities to think about when you next come back.

Chapter 5: A Personal Kaizen

The idea behind Kaizen is is an ongoing, steady effort to make changes to improve the quality of life. The Kaizen approach is never impulsive. Instead, it follows an approach that is long-term and incorporates your personal values when creating your master strategy of your future. The benefit of taking the step of making Kaizen an individual commitment is that it doesn't need to be a quick fix.

It is important to implement changes slowly, but it is important to pay focus on the small details, particularly to those that people consider to be minor. These smaller projects are where you begin building the bigger projects.

Kaizen will help you understand the importance of each step. Most importantly, Kaizen teaches you that each step must be focused toward advancing your goal.

There is never an end to the possibilities of improvement. Westerners were mistaken in their belief that what isn't broken doesn't require any repair. Actually, Kaizen teaches you that there is no alternative but to climb, but you must don't think you've been there.

Once you begin to think that you were begin your journey.

Kaizen is a Japanese concept. Japanese Kaizen is very similar to The Latin Magis. In Chapter 3 both concepts advocate for continuous seeking to learn and improving the quality of one's life. This is about having a belief that regardless of how well you're at present there is always room to improve. There is always the potential for significant improvements. All you need to do is continue to push forward. Retrace your gaze, but do not return.

10 Actions Steps Successful People Follow to Ensure Continuous Improvement

There are many things you can accomplish to increase the quality of your own Kaizen. The previous chapters offered general guidelines for how you can enhance your life. Here's a list of personal habits that you can develop or actions that you can implement to embody the spirit of Kaizen. Kaizen:

(1) Keep both a digital and an analog scrapbook. The term that is used in this case refers to "and," not "or," which means that it is suggested to keep both. If you are documenting your life's important events, you can keep a napkin of your initial date notes from your family members or flowers from

your loved ones. You can keep your scrapbooks full of them. Make sure to be as imaginative as you can and ensure that you include your own personal notes and notes about the mementos that you have chosen to preserve in your scrapbook.

Nowadays, it's possible to snap photos from smartphones. The moments that are not guarded are often the most beautiful , so be sure to add candid pictures of yourself as well as your loved ones in an online scrapbook (or on your social media accounts) that you can access to at any time. These little things can count for a great deal. If you're sad or sad, your scrapbooks remind you that you're not all alone. It can help keep things in perspective particularly during difficult times.

(2)Free you from the shackles that are your comfortable zone. The majority of successful people on the planet have taken the risk of following their passions. Staying in the comfort zone that is your own comfort zone prevents you from being exposed to the outside world. It's okay to be quirky occasionally so long as it makes you feel happy and content. If you're always safe it is unlikely that you'll grow. You shouldn't only be able to experience the splendor of the world in images. You should experience it with all five of your senses.

(3) Be Creative; engage the brain's creative side. Get an instrument and learn to play it. Music keeps your mind clear and calm. Learn sketch or draw. There is no way to tell whether you are gifted or a keen eye.

(4) Take classes. The class could be about any topic. Choose something that you are interested in for example, the culture of a remote nation that you could visit someday. It is also possible to enroll in the photography course. The theory is that photographers are the only ones with the ability to appreciate the beauty of what would have thought to be boring.

(5) Take long walks. This is the most affordable way to expand your perspectives. A long walk will help you escape the monotony of life. Note down your observations and make notes on your own. Take notes on conversations with people. Discover their experiences and expand your knowledge of what the world can provide.

(6) Unplug your devices. This may be the most difficult part for those who are connected to the world of technology. Every now and then

go for a walk or go to a place that you've not been to. It's fine to snap photos to use as a memory entry in your scrapbook. However, make sure you get the most of your time spent. Let your mind go without having to go through a lot of e-mails and messages from your friends.

(7)Schedule an hour of "me" period of time. Create time for activities you can complete at your own pace. Playing games or watching TV doesn't count. Go to your preferred spa and enjoy an indulgence massage.

(8)Watch TED videos or attend Attend a TED event in your area. The speakers at TED events are awe-inspiring and have stories to tell. Make sure you don't have an attitude that you go there to just have fun and laugh. Be aware of the essence of their stories , and keep in mind that someday you will have your own personal story to tell with others and to inspire them.

(9)Teach. The most rewarding aspect of instructing is the fact that you don't just impart what you have learned but also give some of your self to other students. It's time to improve those speaking skills through conducting a seminar or teaching an online class for free.

(10) Do what you are good at. A few people are able to identify their passions, however if you're sure of it you should pursue it and be proficient at it.

Chapter 6: Reach Your Goals With Kaizen

Personal Kaizen is a process-oriented. It's more about the journey, the little challenges that you encounter and how you handle the ones that are more important than the end goal. Kaizen recognizes that you are an ongoing work or a masterpiece in making.

Plan-Do-Study-Act (PDSA)

The PDSA uses a method similar as the 5-step Kaizen method. In reality, this is a form of Kaizen method that was specifically designed to help you develop your habits that will help you realize your goals.

1. Plan

Examine your dreams and make it a plan. Be sure that your goals are based on reality. For instance, there's no way to take on supernatural powers.

Make a concrete goal in your mind. You can't only dream of becoming millionaire, but you can think of becoming a millionaire prior to the time you reach 30.

Create a plan of how you intend to accomplish your goals. Following the same model If you wish to become a millionaire by the time you reach 30 you need to make a commitment to certain behaviors that align with your goals , and eliminate the ones that don't.

Create a plan of action that is clear and precise. Utilizing the same scenario that if you are looking to make it big begin by establishing your own company such as an publishing business. Make a list of ways you intend to start your own business, such as asking your acquaintances to lend your initial capital investment, or getting an advance from the bank or other financial institution, etc.

2. Do

This is a straightforward two-letter word, however this aspect of the method is the most difficult one to accomplish. Certain people are able to go to the point of planning, and when it's time to time to execute they become overwhelmed and then fall back. This is why it's essential to be involved in what you have planned. If not, it could be much easier to back out and put the plan on hold for the time being.

3. Study

The second is often the most difficult, but once you've got through it, the rest is just an issue to making the best decision. This is about assessing the results of the previous step. Analyze your strengths and weaknesses. Conduct a SWOT analysis and then proceed with the following step.

4. Act

In order to remain afloat or even ahead, choosing the right path following is essential. This is the time to take action in response to threats from the outside. How you respond will determine the success of your efforts.

Chapter 7: The Basics Of Kaizen Kaizen

To understand Kaizen to understand it, we need to start by looking at its past to understand the origins of it and the reasons its reasons for being successful. As a business-oriented philosophy, Kaizen was made popular by Masaaki Imai around three years ago. The author of the book introduced the concept and its philosophical concept into the world of management of business as well as in the context of social practices within the wider culture. It is a concept that is primarily grounded in corporate practices, however it is also a possibility to apply in everyday life to help you improve your lifestyle.

It's an Japanese word which, when divided into two, gives meaning. The word Kai refers to "change," and the word Zen refers to "to enhance for the better." When these words are paired and interpreted, it could be read in the sense of "improvement."

Kaizen's historical roots could originate in Japan but its true roots lie within America the manufacturing capabilities and business potential could really take off. In World War II, American producers didn't have the resources or the money to make radical changes to boost production. As a result, they had to rely on minor changes to their work environment to achieve more efficient outcomes. Small changes in the workplace resulted in new adjustments occurring every day and, as workers adapted to these changes and began to work more efficiently and adjust to the changes. This process was then established and is now integral part of nearly every company.

What brought about the popularity of Kaizen was the fact that it was Toyota who released a book about its ideals of manufacturing in 2001. It emphasized how important it is to make incremental improvement within its manufacturing process.

What is Kaizen? It's a system which focuses on more than the greater goal and eventual transformation of the business world and our everyday habits, but instead talks on the necessity of everyday development. According to Kaizen it is imperative to be better each day if we desire to succeed. this method believes that bigger objectives will be fulfilled automatically when every day, small adjustments are made.

The reason for this is fascinating because when you set goals on your own, you are prone to thinking about what's realistically achievable. We all want to set goals and targets which are as huge as they can get and can adversely impact your thoughts because you're always thinking about the best way achieve it. This causes us to not want to get to work as the task we've set ourself is so big that it will require a lot of effort to accomplish it. This is the reason only a handful of people are able to complete such tasks and finish them, while many give up completely.

Kaizen is different in that it requires you to take pleasure in the journey, not focusing on the final goal. If your goal could be completed in a single second, as many people imagine it would be after having thought about it for a while It wouldn't be much enjoyable at all and you'd be learning nothing. When you break the task down into smaller pieces that can be accomplished You'll not only be able be more motivated to finish your tasks , but also notice improvement in yourself as well.. This type of improvement is priceless as it's something that happens throughout the day, which means you'll be able to study the process and take lessons from it. Kaizen can also change the way we approach achieving our objectives. Instead of believing that change will only be achieved through effort and huge steps, it teaches us that it's in these tiny steps that change is created.

If he makes daily small steps the man can eventually reach the top of a peak, however, the only way to do that is when he doesn't overdo to the finish line and become exhausted. A mountain climb isn't about staring at the summit in the hopes of reaching it, and then crying in discomfort when you realize that it's not there. It is much more likely to make it to the summit if you do not think about it and pay attention to each step you take. It will be apparent that every step is enjoyable. When you get focused on the little things your work will become easier to manage and more enjoyable.

Imagine a worker having been instructed by his colleagues that he has to complete the task in a specific way regardless of what it is at the close of the year. He has the direction that he must follow to complete this. After he completes the first step in achieving his goal, he's likely to begin thinking about the additional work that he has to do in order to achieve the goal and how challenging it is to get to the target. This can discourage him from working on the project in front of him. And, not only that, the stress of the greater task can reduce the efficiency and concentration of his employees which can lead to a decline on the level of his work. If he had only focused only on the task before him, without thinking about the bigger picture and objectives, he would have been content to devote all of effort and attention into the work, which would have resulted in more effective results for the company.

The brain also encourages us to feel motivated by looking at the work that is accomplished and reveling in the realization that at the very least a portion of the task was accomplished. If we just concentrate on the bigger picture our brain will never be satisfied. Instead of the tiny steps that we take to encourage us to be more productive and more, they demotivate us as we are constantly being reminded of the insignificantness of the task we've just completed , it is compared to the huge task that remains to be finished. Kaizen advises you to view your small task as an ultimate goal. When you do this your brain stays engaged because each small thing is viewed as a huge accomplishment. Do this each day so that your self-esteem can increase substantially.

Kaizen is also a way to ensure that every day, there is a the goal of achieving it and you'll end each day feeling like you've gained just a tiny bit. The success of any company depends on the performance of its employees and it's only when employees improve day-to-day that the company will do also improve. The result is that Kaizen can help you concentrate on what's ahead of you. It makes you feel more at ease and inspired, which eventually results in a boost in productivity and achievement of the bigger target.

The heart of Kaizen

Five fundamental principles form the foundation of Kaizen:

* Be aware of your customers

It will flow.

* Head to Gemba
* empower people
* Be honest.

Five of these concepts when implemented in concert each day, will allow constant improvement to occur within the business.

Know who your customer is

Everything in Kaizen begins with the customer. If you are able to get the attention of your client and provide precisely what they want then you'll be successful. The aim of any business is to discover what customers are looking for and ensure they improve their experience by offering them satisfactory products. Growth in the business via Kaizen can be easily assessed by the degree to which the organization can create value for its customers.

Let it flow

Kaizen is also focused on reducing waste within the company. It considers all things valuable and waste is the cause of the company's inability to succeed. If daily tasks are planned in the Kaizen system, the primary aim is to ensure that no resource is wasted and most value is derived from every possible source.

Go to Gemba

Gemba is where everything happens typically referred to as the home. This is a rule that all managers should follow in the course of each day. It is essential to be aware of the areas where work is producing value and know what's happening in your own workplace.

Empower People

Kaizen can't be effective without everyone knowing what steps to do. If there is no communication within the team, no one can do the job required, and be focused on the larger goals instead of the small steps. A highly-engaged group is one where everyone trusts one another and communication is open to ensure that everyone is aware of what needs to be done.

Be Transparent

Kaizen is not effective unless employees are aware of the bigger goals that will be achieved at the close each year. It's not enough to continue making small improvements without checking to see if the results impact the overall productivity of your company. Management must make sure that they are armed with the right information and publish it frequently for all to see.

PDCA Cycle

Kaizen can be attained by making sure that it is achieved when the PDCA cycle is repeatedly repeated. This is the Plan-Do-Check-Act cycle that is also referred to in the Deming cycle. This cycle makes sure that every worker is motivated to encourage them to achieve greater productivity. This process ensures that there is a continuous improvement in terms of the amount and the caliber of work, while simultaneously cutting down on costs at each step. This is basically a bigger improvements to the business will only occur when each day we review the process of work in order to improve the quality, decrease the loss, and gain additional value for the materials that we have. Kaizen ultimately, when paired with this cycle, will lead to everyone working in harmony so that production processes are scrutinized to ensure that productivity is improved as much as is feasible.

Plan

The first step of the entire process is to organize everything in a systematic manner. You must decide on the main production theme for the business is, the products you're creating and how you're making it. The theme is crucial because it informs your employees how their work should flow and what they should be required to do. It also helps everyone comprehend the production process and also to spot difficulties. Then, you can study both the material and financial state of the business and think of innovative ways to accomplish tasks. Determine what the tasks you will be assigned to be, then identify the trouble areas, and then conduct an study of these areas to make sure that you understand what the root cause is, and then begin working to find solutions to the issues.

Do

Once you've done the research The next step is to determine what needs to be accomplished. Make a checklist of steps that should be put into place throughout the company to increase productivity.

Check

Once you've established standards for the measures to be followed by the company, this step is about making sure whether the process is in order and is being adhered to.

Act

In this stage it is necessary to establish a standard for the measures to ensure that the work can be done in a continuous manner. Re-evaluate all measures in accordance with the ones that have proven successful, and evaluate everything within the company.

When when the PDCA Cycle is completed, it is time to move into following the SDCA Cycle. While the first cycle is focused on the improvement of all aspects within the company, the second one is focused on maintenance. After you've identified every flaw in the work environment, you must to establish a standard for what needs to be done to ensure you can have a set of guidelines on which you are able to determine the effectiveness of each task that are being carried out. This S in the last sentence is for standardization, and the notion of support since this cycle is regarded as the pillar which helps to ensure the daily operation of the company.

The importance of standardization is in the success of any company because it provides an opportunity to evaluate the efficiency of the production process. It is difficult to know how you're doing without certain standards to measure on. It also allows your employees to be aware of how to complete their work and what the most efficient method of completing the job is. Additionally the moment new employees join to your company it will be simpler to teach them as you'll have a strong base to require them to adhere to. The standards also ensure that there's no variation in the work environment as everyone knows what they need to do and how to ensure that each task is done exactly. This can prevent mistakes from occurring because any deviation is easy to identify and rectify.

Kaizen's history Kaizen

The term Kaizen was a worldwide phenomenon that received acclaim through

Masaaki Imai's writings. Masaaki Imai (born 1930) is an Japanese management scholar and board expert, specifically , on Kaizen and is renowned for his work in quality control. Kaizen Institute Consulting Group (KICG) Kaizen Institute Consulting Group (KICG) began to be formed in the year 1985 to enable western institutions to comprehend the principles of Kaizen and the ways they can be applied across cultures.

Kaizen was developed in various Japanese firms that had at one time or another, learned leadership techniques and skills that were inherited from United States and even from Europe. The strategies were created under the guidance of a handful of influential companies who are accountable to improve efficiency and productivity.

The beginning of Kaizen dates all the way to World War II when Japanese enterprises first began to implement effective production cycles employing this method. They became the first to incorporate the Kaizen philosophy in their production. The concept was influenced to some extent by American instructors in quality and business who visited Japan. Through the 50s this groundbreaking concept became extremely popular in Japan and today the majority of modern businesses follow this approach due to its efficacy.

After World War II, during the period of economic reconstruction Japan's products were viewed as cheap, but poor quality. In order to reverse this type of bad press it was necessary to increase efficiency and quality began as well as one of the groups that played an integral part in the film included JUSE, the Union of Japanese Scientists and Engineers (JUSE). They held a variety of workshops on the use of statistics in management and quality assurance for large companies, and executives at times. Through these efforts, businesses began to recognize the importance of quality management and began to work towards building factories that are world class. At each stage of development, organizations that were voluntary were created to implement various workplace improvement initiatives, some of that included garbage disposal (Muda-Dori) and cost efficiency and industrial safety management, the reduction of defects and 5S (which we'll talk about later) and the creation Quality circles. Quality circles are groups of employees performing similar jobs which meet on a regular basis to analyze, comprehend and decide on workplace issues. Quality circles are the identical to the PDCA Cycle however, it is conducted by employees rather than management.

In 1955 in 1955, in 1955, JPC (Japan Productivity Center) was formed by labor unions, groups and academics as well as businesses. JPC was the leader of the growth campaign and eventually became an international organization. Since 1955 in the year 1955, the JPC has been able to send several teams for industrial tours to various modern manufacturing facilities across developed nations including those in the U.S., to study their effectiveness and development strategies. The outcomes were then shared during feedback sessions that were held throughout the nation, and further gathered for distribution to companies interested in the subject. This strategy helped in the enhancement of quality and efficiency within Japanese companies in general.

In the course of focusing on improving the standard of their products from a perspective of production, manufacturing quality items and service, a significant number of Japanese enterprises launched various initiatives to improve performance and efficiency as a method of implementing a successful business strategy. The concept of TQC (Total Quality Control) was created at this point. Numerous high-ranking corporations in Japan like Yamaha, Sony, Honda, Canon, Nissan, Panasonic, Toyota, and Suzuki continuously pushed for universal implementation to Total Quality Control. This has enabled them to rise to the top of the line in manufacturing and development.

A number of private and public sectors implemented these measures and broadened the scope of these measures. The measures soon were not restricted to the manufacturing industry and were also used to increase the loyalty of customers. The Kaizen modification attracted the attention of a few American as well as European corporate managers, academics, and engineers who travelled to Japan to study the key elements of Japanese firms' capacity to enhance their business. Then, many firms then took Japanese manufacturing and production management expertise and know-how and organized them in accordance with to the American as well as European business environment.

As mentioned earlier the quality and manufacturing techniques were first brought by Japan. The manufacturing methods and quality were first introduced from the U.S. to Japan and were modified as time went through and improved by Japanese producers in response to their different dimensions, markets, environment for production and various other aspects.

TPS

TPS (Toyota Production System) is a well-known established management system. TPS is built on two fundamental concepts : the Jidoka and the Just-In-Time. The Jidoka can be used to immediately stop an inoperable system, thereby preventing the production of defective goods. In contrast it is the Just-In-Time technique is founded on making only what is required to avoid the production of excessive quantities of items. At simultaneously, making sure that the right raw materials are kept in stock for a seamless manufacturing process.

To elaborate further the fundamentals upon which TPS is built:

Jidoka

Jidoka is all about drawing and visualizing issues to ensure that they don't get buried however, everyone can be aware of them, ensuring that problems can be quickly addressed. It is based on the notion that the worth of a product or entire company is determined by how manufacturing happens. For instance in the event that a malfunctioning component is discovered or a machine malfunctions, that device will stop working immediately and force the workers to stop manufacturing and require them to react and correct the issue.

What exactly does this mean? It means that the system is stopped until normal operation can be restored. It also guarantees that, if an issue with equipment occurs or there's a problem with service The machines cease by themselves and can identify the issue, and after that only products that meet the specifications for quality are able to be produced. Since the system stops automatically when there is a problem and it's reported on the notice boards with visuals (ondon). This allows users to keep researching other systems , and also to identify what could be the cause of the problem to prevent their occurrence.

This means that several operators are in charge of the machines they have in the company which will result in greater efficiency while in the same time, permitting for continuous and endless changes which will result in greater productivity.

Just-in-Time

This is a method for the improvement of quality. It permits the production of only the products that are considered important and in the amount needed. The components that are manufactured and delivered are required to meet the standards of quality already established by the manufacturer. this is accomplished via Jidoka. Development of high-quality goods through this particular process is successful because it removes the waste, unrealistic requirements in the production line or even inconsistencies, greater profits can be made. For instance when a client wants to receive their new car as they desire it and when they want it, the car has to be produced efficiently at the time it is required. This means that the manufacturing process has to be efficient as well as efficient so that the process could be completed in a short time.

Masaki Imai has stated that Kaizen is a broader concept that encourages continuous growth of an organization's operations. It is said that the work of change never ends for any company since their current systems are always being questioned, every minute.

What made this strategy well-known? It became famous when Toyota employed it to establish itself as the leader of the automotive world. Instead of just pursuing big projects, the Toyota employees were encouraged to be aware of the challenges facing the company however small they could appear. They were given the opportunity to identify the root of the problems and discover the most effective solutions to them, too.

The Japanese industrial sector typically follows two strategies. This is the method of empirical analysis, which is focused on processing data and the bottom-up method which is run by a community group that is part of the Quality Control Process. The goal of this approach is to ensure that the information of the business is concealed. Any issues must come to the surface and be dealt with promptly. Bottom-up approaches ensure that employees are engaged in their work that is why they take care of their jobs rather than apathy that could cause manufacturing errors. This is the primary reason behind the achievement of Japanese firms : they treat their workers with respect, reward them with enough and provide them with a solid reason to be invested in their job. The entire organization is made up of people, not equipment.

In the wake of the numerous program of efficiency and quality improvement implemented by a large number of Japanese companies the production rates of their firms have improved from being poor to exceptional which has made Japan"the "nation of world-class quality."

Let's consider an example: in the year 1990 in the year 1990, an MIT (Massachusetts Institute of Technology) study group studied The Toyota Production Process to identify areas of competitive advantage for Japanese automobile manufacturers. They then released a book titled "The Machine That Changes the world." In the volume, TPS was expanded on then reorganized and named"Lean Manufacturing. "Lean manufacturing system." This method was later criticized by the researchers they believed that a bottom-up strategy is superior to an approach that is bottom-up.

Then, General Electric (GE) Company has further enhanced it. The Kaizen method has been extended to the entire manufacturing system to ensure improvement throughout the entire process. It is the "Six Sigma" and lean manufacturing technique and later joined into "Lean as well as Six Sigma," have been integrated into Kaizen and have become an example of efficiency in the west and product innovation in the modern day.

The core of Kaizen is that people working in all positions of the business are who are the most knowledgeable about their work and, by showing trust in their capabilities, managing the project is enhanced to a higher degree than what was initially possible. This unique project that is collaborative encourages innovation and change as allowing for change. Both are available to all workers. To make progress more efficient be made, every barrier needs to be removed. Kaizen is a method of thinking for everyone, not only the method of ensuring manufacturing profitability. This is because everyone is involved in making changes. By dissecting issues, analysing every aspect, and making adjustments as needed, Kaizen helps make the task easier for everyone. Kaizen does not just apply to one person , but it must be a part of everyone in the organization since everyone is a member which means that each play a part. To everyone, Kaizen must become an method of continuous improvement for them as well as the business.

There are three main Kaizen principles, according to Masaki Imai. He stated that the organization's management and employees must be able to work together to meet the basic standards. He suggests three primary aspects that should be taken into consideration for the efficiency of this process, which include the administrative role of the visual, of the leader of the organization as well as the growth of a business that depends on experience and education.

Kaizen's Pillars

Housekeeping

The workplace is called Gemba In Japanese. This approach is primarily focused on the transformational process of managing work. Gemba is a term used to describe the workplace. Gemba was established to be an environment where value is added to the product as well as the service it provides before it is moved to the next stage of production. In this regard it was a technical framework utilized. They are also known by the 5S.

The idea was derived from the Japanese words "first characters" that correspond to the five words. The list is five guidelines for creating the safe and healthy working setting. The five S comprise of Seiri (organization), Seiso (purity), Shitsuke (discipline), Seiketsu (cleanliness) as well as Seiton (tidiness).

The 5S's English definition can be summated in the form of arranging the workplace, straighten it out, clean the office, clean it, and keep it. The 5S provides information on the way a workplace is. Specific standards have to be adhered to by non-manufacturing and manufacturing companies that include cleanliness, health and ergonomics. In the Five S, Five S involves analyzing employee opinions about a manufacturing facility as well as the entire company as well as the entire company. It is now an essential tool for any manufacturing company. The 5S method lets manufacturing companies achieve the top of the line.

The 5S

The 5S refer to:

Seiri

Seiri means separating the things that aren't essential from what is. Utilize methods like red tags to label items that you don't consider to be essential to this. Everyone should be able to judge whether the items are required or not before they are taken away. Anything that is marked red should be offered for sale, raffled off or sold to employees, thrown away, or donated for scrap to recyclers.

Seiton

Seiton is designed to draw attention to the objects that should be preserved and secured. The goal is to make these objects evident. Materials should be marked and marked to make it easy to identify them by their place. It is based on law that every item has a proper location, and employees should be able to envision the appropriate places.

Seiso

Seiso means to scrub whatever is left. It is important to ensure that they are clean painting them to create an eye-catching and pleasing appearance.

Seiketsu

Seiketsu is a part of the daily distribution and testing. When there's a shift in one of the company's selected Kaizen fields, every employee would like to know about it, too. It is important to provide them with the necessary training and make sure that everyone has access all the relevant information regarding these changes.

Shitsuke

Shitsuke is about standardization as well as discipline. First, establish a regular schedule. Also, make sure that you make use of your time off to tidy and straighten up your space of work.

There are many other benefits to the 5S system, including:

* The creation of healthy, welcoming and safe workplaces for employees

It helps to rejuvenate the employees and increases the productivity of employees and boosts morale in the organization.

* Cuts down on time wastage by removing the need to look for equipment. This makes the operator's task very simple.

It can help reduce working hours and also frees space in the work area.

It helps create a feeling of belonging to the workplace and also builds a sense of solidarity between the employees that creates a sense that they belong to a community of caring.

Waste Disposal

The term "waste" is Muda and is referred to as Muda in Japanese. It is a term used to describe things which do not contribute value to the workplace. Work is described as an array of activities which add an added value. There are many things to consider, ranging from the components of the final product to raw materials that aren't adding value, but instead cause more issues. Here are a few examples of the waste a company produces:

* Overproduction, defective components in inventory, parts that aren't neededly transported and inspections that impede production.

Routing documents, inefficient paperwork and signature certificates workers accumulating a lot of documents and files that are buried, inefficient information, and the transmission of work that is prone to error are all considered to be office waste.

Seven Deadly Wastes Seven Deadly Wastes

Overproduction

This can happen when machine failure employees' absence, machine failure, and the rejection of staff and employees occur.

Sometimes, the effort to keep pace with production could result in huge waste. This also leads to wasteful consumption of human resources and utilities and increased interest burdens. the consumption of raw materials long before they are required, high cost of transportation and administrative costs and more space than is needed to store inventory that is not needed and other items.

Motion

Any type of employee activity that doesn't add value to the production process is thought of as unproductive. Staff members should avoid lifting or carrying things which require significant strength and effort as it can be risky, dangerous and a sign of activities that are not value-adding. The organization of work spaces can be a great way to reduce the amount of human movements.

Deficiencies

Rejection of goods, and their later reproduction are excellent examples of the duplication of time and expense. The rejections could require more time for repairs, as well as more time on inspection, and requiring workers to be always on standby to shut down the machine when instructed to do so. It can also increase the amount of the amount of paperwork.

Waiting

It happens when operators are inactive. This is referred to as waiting because the operator's work is delayed due to the absence of small components or downtime, and it causes a waste of time. The lead time in manufacturing begins when the business is able to pay for the materials that are required for the production of the item. It is completed when the business receives the payment from consumers for the particular product. The term "leap time" refers to cash turnover. If there is a short lead time, this means that resources are being utilized efficiently. There is an impressive level of flexibility to meet customer requirements and a comparatively small amount is spent on operations. Waste disposal is an extremely important tool in Kaizen. Other types of waste in this category are documents, items and other information that are dormant and don't add benefit to the manufacturing process and at the same time costing companies in the maintenance.

Inventory

Inventory waste includes semi-finished products such as end products,, and component materials that remain in the inventory, but aren't adding value to the company or the item's production in the first place; it simply costs money. As they occupy the space they take up, it adds to the operating costs. they need more equipment and facilities, like forklifts and computerized conveyor systems as well as storage units. If these items are kept for a long period of time the quality begins to decline. in terms of quality. As the demand for them increases, customers tend to prefer new items. As new products are introduced and these products are discontinued, they get old news. Storage units also require more operational management and personnel. They are also susceptible to destruction or disasters through fire. To address this issue to avoid this, the Just-In-Time development technique previously mentioned must be implemented and formally incorporated.

Processing

There are many ways waste may form during processing. One example is that every process struggles to sync. It is possible to avoid this by requiring a redesign of the assembly line to reduce input consumption and produce the same output required.

The types of inputs are equipment, materials and energy. the output is the requested products or services that are to be delivered with added value and yield. The process of redesigning the assembly line is cutting down on the number of employees working on the line, as the less workers, the fewer mistakes that could be made. This can reduce the quality of products since only educated employees remain in the process. It doesn't necessarily have to make other employees dismissed. They could be allocated to different output areas. With increased productivity and the output increases, there will be savings. The need for additional employees is likely to be in the manufacturing industry with a long production line. Therefore, this could also lead to more work-in-process time, which would mean a longer lead time.

The chance of making errors increases with more employees, which can lead to the development of quality issues. In the end, longer lead time as well as inefficient equipment, a larger number of employees, and new employees who have no formal training will lead to higher production costsand lower profits.

Transportation

Transportation involves the utilization of forklifts, trucks and conveyors in production industries. It is an vital aspect of manufacturing but the transportation of the materials doesn't add value to the finished product. Additionally, there is always a chance of damages during transportation, therefore any part of the production line that seems to be distant from the mainline, should be moved closer to mainline to prevent wasted materials.

Chapter 8: Kaizen And Business

Another important goal you could make use of Kaizen for is to establish and expand your company. Rome was not founded in a single day and a company doesn't emerge from the ground in a flash. In fact, even if your company has been established, it will always require improvement incrementallyto establish your brand and keep growing. This is why Kaizen is focused on "gradual advancement" and is designed to ensure that businesses endure.

Have you ever dreamed of launching your own business? What kept you from doing exactly that? Was it because you is consumed by your family obligations or day job or other responsibilities that you have to attend to? It is not for everyone to be a businessperson. If you think this career path is yours, then what should you do to achieve it?

Take a moment to think about this: Pick the right time each day to take a seat and imagine what your company will look like. Then, take a moment to visualize yourself as a businessperson. You should ask yourself these questions: what will it be that you'll create? Where will you market it? How many employees would you need to employ? Where can you find suppliers?

The exercise will accomplish two things:

* Now you'll be more focused on launching your business idea.

Your mind will begin to look for the answers, and you will be able to find the materials needed.

We're aiming with Kaizen is to slowly introduce you to this innovative approach: small amounts each day can result in greater shifts. Consider the most sensible measure or action you could take to bring your dreams to life:

Perhaps you can start by giving yourself an hour per day to research the field you're considering.

* Make an effort to meet every day one person who is already operating within your field, that might be able help you set up your business.

• Meet with businessmen who support your idea for a business and ask them their thoughts on it , and the methods they used to succeed.

There's no reason to leave your job before you're ready to start your own company. Even if you are still working professionally elsewhere, even small actions can still be accomplished. The details of your financial strategy will determine how quickly you'll be able to achieve your goals. Keep in mind that with Kaizen every concept is divided into smaller ideas. That's evidently the reason it's an effective method to take small steps (weekly and monthly) toward your goal. This will allow you to move with ease instead of a sprint. It's this consistency that can ultimately lead to the growth of your company regardless of what type of speed you'd like to expand at.

Expanding your business

If you currently run an organization (or are in the position of a supervisor) and you are in a supervisory position, then having the Kaizen approach to life definitely will pay off. It is ideal when you are able to put the Kaizen principle into your personal and professional life. Your employees must be committed to Kaizen to fully integrate it into your business. Here are some ideas for creating an "Kaizen workplace":

Examine the most important Business Best Practices

Begin by identifying the business areas that are vital to the achievement of your company. These could include production, procurement sales, or even helping customers. Every month, you should try to convince employees to concentrate on one major goal for every branch of the company. It could be something likethis "This month, we're planning to increase our customer base by at minimum 10." This could mean the improvement of your manufacturing capabilities as well as customer service and marketing requirements. Additionally, you need to establish an annual goal to grow your business which includes each department.

Find the Daily Activities

Find three activities a day that your sales team must be doing regularly to achieve this objective. For example, you could explain to them that if they want to increase the market share of your company They should do:

Contact five satisfied customers each day and ask them if they have any suggestions for others who might have an interest in our products.

* Send the existing subscribers an update via email and inform them of the most recent updates we could send them in the coming quarter.

* Post on our company's website one blog update each day to inform people of and learn about the latest innovations in our services.

Naturally, any activities you decide to perform are contingent on your business. However, the goal is to keep the whole organization working regularly on the most significant projects and reaching monthly goals. The routine, gradual steps influenced by Kaizen can keep employees on track each morning and avoid becoming lost in the essential elements to an efficient work day.

Utilizing Kaizen to build an Team Spirit

If the team is motivated the team's efficiency increases. A person who is involved in business processes is more likely take on new ideas that can work for the company. The feeling of team spirit is the feeling of unity employees feel and makes them feel more connected to their jobs and colleagues, their company and their work. When employees feel as if they're part of something bigger than themselves this makes them feel satisfied. If they feel satisfied they're more likely to perform more effectively. They also become selfless, and they'll begin to assist others in their work or do more work in order to see the company's growth.

If you are looking for loyal employees, you need to get started developing the team spirit. But, you cannot develop team spirit by taking everyone to lunch once or twice a week. It is essential to create a sense that they're all alike and share the same thoughts. To foster this feeling of belonging, purchase matchy cups, t-shirts and other items that make them feel like they're part the team. Things are a reflection of our emotions and we create meaning through the things we use them for. By providing people with items that bring them back to the group they're part of, you'll help keep their feeling of belonging to the team.

You cannot manage your employees, so you must accept that. The only thing you can do is dictate what they should do, and give them the tools needed to achieve it, and then hope they will succeed. If you try to set the standard for what your employees must do every day this can cause frustration or anger and even demotivation. If you let them do whatever they want to do, employees begin to feel that they can trust you. The most effective motivator for the majority of people is to let them to push themselves. If you demonstrate your faith in their abilities , and then allow them to be themselves they'll be more inclined to challenge themselves to prove they're worthy of your confidence.

Three Kaizen actions that you can apply to help motivate the team are:

* Assign work (which are to be completed by every team members) on an ongoing, monthly, or weekly basis. Allow each employee to inquireand explain truthfully, "why" they have been given their specific duties. This should allow them to feel valued and confident to perform their duties.

Do not assign the responsibility of your employees automatically, with no form of training or preparation. Plan a thorough training and preparation for your employees and for your employees. Even a brief, periodic time of training will be effective in preparing employees for the responsibilities they will face.

* The last stage is the most crucial one. The gradual improvement in productivity of employees is a sure thing when you connect the positive behavior you desire with a system of reward. Be aware that you aren't firing workers who are not performing. You're just motivating your employees to perform better and reward them for their achievements.

It is not a financial gain, however. The research conducted by the Federal Reserve found that monetary incentives can reduce the effectiveness of employees as they start seeing their work solely as a result of financial rewards. Instead, employ other strategies to meet the needs of employees' emotional well-being. The most effective way to motivate employees is to reward and appreciate. The majority of people aren't convinced of their own abilities, and need external validation in order to feel that they are important. Many people want confidence from people who are in charge and who's word is more important in their minds that their personal. When you reward and acknowledge people by giving them a reward, you establish incentives that encourages people to do their best. Both of these actions create a sense of competition between employees. If this contest is healthy, it will serve as a motivator in your workers.

You must reward people who do good and outstanding work with recognition tokens, for example, certificates, medals or even rewards. When you give souvenirs to individuals, be sure to note the specific event as well as their name and any other details that make the award for them. They must feel valued and heard. Additionally ensure that you don't simply distribute these things to everybody as it is an exclusive item that makes people want to work to earn it.

It is important to recognize and recognize good work in the work community by celebrating your successes as a group. Make sure to highlight work anniversary celebrations, individual milestones, or even personal occasions like birthdays or other special occasions. In order to ensure that your team is content and they feel appreciated and valued.

Kaizen Event

An Kaizen event is conducted by a company for solely the aim of improving. It's a brief event that generally only lasts for several days. It's referred to as an event since everyone in the company is expected to be involved and be educated about Kaizen. It doesn't just teach employees about Kaizen and the best way to implement it, but also serves as an assessment that examines the working of the company in order to discover areas for improvement. Although Kaizen is a method of making small steps each day, the goal of an Kaizen occasion is to establish the foundation for the remainder throughout the entire year. When the Kaizen event is held the participants are taught what they need to accomplish and what to concentrate on and at the same as addressing any possible questions. This is how Kaizen can be integrated into the daily operations of the business, and each day following the event, little actions can be implemented to increase the efficiency of the business.

The majority of the work is performed by skilled Kaizen experts who a business must employ. It's a joint effort that's why the business must also set up an Kaizen team which is taught by consultants from outside. When the event is finished the Kaizen team will then assume the responsibility of the event and make sure that everyone is following the principles they were taught at the time of the event.

After an Kaizen event has been conducted the majority of companies ignore the event and do not bother anymore. This is not a good idea since the benefits achieved through the event will end immediately and won't be carried over throughout the year. If you wish the benefits that you will reap from Kaizen to last it is essential to make sure that your team is taking Kaizen seriously. If your employees return to the way they were working, your benefits could be reversed in a short time, meaning that you've just missed a huge chance.

The event itself could result in a significant increase in efficiency and productivity by educating workers on the different programs offered under Kaizen. For example, by educating employees how to cut down on waste the event can increase your profits by between thirty and forty percent. What's required from you is that your employees are open to listening and willing to accept the changes that they are being asked to make since otherwise, they'll take the advice of trainers from Kaizen trainers and then forget about the topic. The Kaizen program should concentrate on other areas besides manufacturing. You could ask your sales and service staff attend several sessions with Kaizen trainers to discover how to deal with their issues by using the Kaizen method of breaking everything into smaller parts.

These are steps to follow in order to run the Kaizen event:

Learn or hire Kaizen Leaders

It is essential to have an individual who can be in charge of the event in order for it to succeed. Kaizen is just like every other method of management that requires the person who is training to be able to effectively communicate the Kaizen concept to employees. Also, it needs to be one who understands the process they are using. Find someone who is knowledgeable about the lean approach and is aware of the way Kaizen is done. If you're not able to afford to employ someone, begin to research and then conduct the Kaizen exercise yourself.

Earn your Trust of the Senior Management

If you're looking to make sure that the changes that you're making to your company's structure are effective, you must to make sure that your top management team is on board. This means that you must to get them to understand the significance of Kaizen and the reasons why they need to commit themselves to.

Find an Game Plan

First, you must establish the limits of the Kaizen event. You must be specific about which areas of your job that you would like to include in Kaizen. Are you focusing on the manufacturing aspect or is it the office too? Are you looking for the secretaries to be educated on Kaizen also? The scope of the event will depend on your requirements. If you believe that there's an the area which has been unprofitable, unruly and inefficient, then it should be included into this Kaizen event. Additionally, you should to ensure that all participants are involved in every Kaizen workshop. The top management should know what the workers in the manufacturing are getting told since this will help them understand what Kaizen can increase profits, and which specific guidelines must be implemented in order to achieve this goal.

It is also important to establish the mission statement of the event. What do you would like to implement to your business? Do you wish to educate your employees about the 5S method? Or do you simply need them to identify ways to improve their work every day? It is essential to be able to communicate with your team members when you are trying to integrate Kaizen within the workplace. You must remember that the majority of your employees may not be aware about Kaizen at all and if you try to confuse them more you'll not be particularly excited about performing the work you ask to.

An Kaizen event will only be successful if everyone is thrilled about the possibility of this new concept. It is important for your employees to implement Kaizen beyond the workplace. The goal of Kaizen is always to show people how to handle any challenge if they break it down into smaller pieces.

Kaizen Training

Kaizen Training involves teaching the entire company about the method and training them for the gradual changes they'll be expected to implement daily. The process begins at the top management of the company . They need to comprehend the reasons why Kaizen is crucial and how it can be interpreted in terms of their roles within the organization to grasp its meaning. Kaizen is ultimately a way of thinking that will only be successful carried out when everyone is excited by the potential of Kaizen.

Top Management Training

Top Management Attitude

The primary components of executive level must be devoted in Kaizen and the Kaizen cause and be effective leaders in the advancement in Kaizen operations. The idea of demanding results right after having Implemented Kaizen without actually taking part with any activities won't improve the morale of employees however, a plethora of poor outcomes will be generated and cause further issues. Top managers must be able of highlighting the essential points with their actions to ensure the success of Kaizen. The most important things they need to impart to the entire workforce are the following: What is Kaizen? What is the difference between creativity and Kaizen? What are the advantages Kaizen offer? What are the best methods to measure Kaizen results? What methods and processes are in use for tracking and implementing Kaizen actions?

Steps that the top executives should do to show their commitment to Kaizen

* Start Meeting: It signifies the announcement made to every employee in the company of the official launch of Kaizen operations by the most senior executives. This demonstrates the deep commitment of the top executives towards Kaizen and can lead to an increase in the motivation of employees since they will realize that their bosses are working to increase the

efficiency of the company's production and efficiency.

* Selecting and supporting Kaizen Leaders: Help can be provided through the rapid choice and approval to Kaizen leaders, approval to perform other Kaizen activities within the working timeframe, and any other assistance that is available. This will enable the entire company to be aware of the significance of Kaizen.

* On-site security This includes going to shop floors to gather information on the climate of the workplace and also the maintenance of equipment. The top managers must be aware of what is happening and, even more important they must demonstrate that they are prepared to inspect anytime to ensure that workers are always alert.

* Appreciation to attend Kaizen gatherings: Participation in Kaizen will show how much the top management team is committed to Kaizen and related changes. Employees must observe all this and be excited by the process.

* The amount of money required to fund Kaizen One important aspect of Kaizen is the

ability to make use of the existing resources within the organization , without forcing an organization to undertake huge investment. Kaizen typically requires relatively little effort when it comes to major purchases, and it does not incur additional expenses. Instead, it lowers expenses.

The top managers are the ones who diagnose Top managers should regularly receive information of team members of the QCC (Quality Control) team, and then assess the state of the Kaizen initiatives. It's also an excellent chance for the employees to listen to what the thoughts of the most senior executives are. It's a crucial juncture to create a bridge between the workers and management.

A reward system that rewards that is given to a person or group is offered due to the fact that they have produced amazing results that have helped to achieve the steadyness in Kaizen execution. The reward could be anything including recognition from peers of a gift card or even cash. Everyone would like to be acknowledged in different ways. Some people prefer being rewarded while others need an email. It is important to modify your system of recognition to meet the specific needs of your employees.

It is essential to establish an education program prior to attempting to provide training specifically targeted for Kaizen executives to ensure that the highest-ranking executives are aware of the above mentioned activities. This will not only allow them to gain a greater understanding of Kaizen however, it will also enable them to share their knowledge and to discuss issues with top company managers. This can lead to an environment of collaboration where the data and results are shared to help improve Kaizen methods.

Instructing and creating Kaizen Leaders

The role of Kaizen Leaders

Kaizen leaders leadership role in Kaizen actions, which includes enforcing the recommendations of both Basic and Advanced Trainers. Dedication and leadership are among the primary factors that determine the efficiency of Kaizen activities. Kaizen leaders have to accomplish the following:

Kaizen leaders should be the ones who implement Kaizen methods under the supervision of the Kaizen Trainer(s). The things they could do include:

* Project QCC Quality control circles are an organization of employees supervised by an Kaizen leader that makes sure that Kaizen practices like no waste, continuous changes and fixing manufacturing flaws are regularly implemented.

* Guidance during QCC leadership selection

* Assisting QCC individuals or teams with poor or inactive activities.

Another task they must accomplish is to create plans for events, annual plan of action, instructional plans technology plans, budget plans, design internal posters, create brochures and badges, and so on. This is essential for the creation of Kaizen actions and to secure prior approval from the top management to carry out Kaizen associated tasks. They also have to gather progress reports and present these to the top managers in every Kaizen operations. They must also be involved in preparing talks, making presentations, and verifying data, and also leading meetings or conferences which are focused on Kaizen.

The training of Kaizen Leaders

The capability and knowledge in the hands of Kaizen Leaders can be developed with the help of the Kaizen leadership activities listed below:

* Sharing their knowledge on the challenges encountered in Kaizen training in open group discussions. This will assist the whole organisation as the challenges they confront are likely to be faced by the personnel of the entire company. By addressing these issues in the earliest possible time they can be resolved and the underlying issues solved.

* Announcing Kaizen-related activities

* Mentoring and training provided through Basic Trainers or Intermediate Trainers and Kaizen Experts.

Presenting at workshops and conferences about Kaizen.

Total Quality Management (TQM)

Kaizen refers to a concept used to describe a system that encompasses programs and practices including recommendations by employees and TQM. What exactly is TQM?

It's a term that is focused on improving efficiency in the workplace across the entire business. Total Quality Management includes health and quality control, employee engagement and cost management, improved efficiency, and improving performance. The people are the key to the performance in the TQM cycle and it is emphasized since it's the component of Kaizen in which everyone takes part. The most common practices in TQM are things like the preparation of meetings, coordination chance creation, and participation on the job.

The TQM procedure is concerned with the cross-functional leadership of an organization and growth of the company, as well as the efficiency of the company's increase. TQM can be used as an approach and resource for improving the potential of individuals and success in the workplace.

TQM incorporates current development programs and common management strategies and cutting-edge methods into an organized approach that is that focuses on improvement in quality. In the end, these efforts are targeted towards a rise in satisfaction with the customer. It is important to emphasize is the fact that the technological elements of change could be technological or mechanical. Change is not a lot to be associated with people and is only tied to the relationships they have with technological advancements. That means that changing individuals doesn't help in fostering innovations. It's when the way they work and interact with machines are changed that innovation happens.

To maximize profits and to improve quality and efficiency An organization must unlock the potential in its workforce by enticing employees to complete their work correctly from the beginning. This also allows the high-level managers to communicate to each employee that each and every employee is expected to be dedicated and put in constant effort to improve the efficiency of the whole company. When the employees are aware of this, they'll be more motivated as they recognize how vital they are to the achievement of the company.

The workplace must be an environment where each employee is motivated to meet the goals of the company. If employees are pressured into work they will end having no interest in the tasks they're performing which can negatively impact productivity. It also gives the management the chance to look at any suggestions that come from employees who are motivated and can be a part of the success of the company. The top management simply streamlining orders and prioritizing downwards to employees and permitting ideas to flow upwards. This is an automated self-checking process because, as orders decrease and workers are notified, they are able to float any issues that might be affecting the order back up to ensure that top management is able to resolve them.

The TQM methodology provides specific strategies to increase the effectiveness of the business. It accomplishes this by studying the manner in which work is carried out from a systematic, structured continuous, operational, and consistent perspective. The principal objective for Total Quality Management is to: Total Quality Management method is to:

* Respond to all foreign and domestic consumer demands.

• Involve all operational entities within the company and make sure that there is no one left outside the area of discussion.

• Understanding the effect of heterogeneity on TQM processes and possible methods of improving these processes.

* Highlight the continuous growth of Kaizen.

• Employee engagement and motivation to become the main driving force in increasing effectiveness and profitability.

If there isn't tolerance or patience during this TQM period, the result will always be disappointment and discontent. Collaboration and cooperation are essential to the growth and success of the company. It is evident that engagement among employees and manufacturing processes that are process-oriented are crucial elements and, thus, are the fundamental elements of TQM. The team's structure and procedures are crucial to improving the quality of each member and enhancing the ability of the organization to implement these procedures during every Kaizen session.

The TQM approach to organizational improvement is like the Kaizen method of improvement. The components and features of both are co-operative and could require a single organizational framework. Combining them is the most effective strategy for successful organization.

Quality Cost, Delivery, and Quality (QCD)

It is widely acknowledged that consumers rule the world in an economy that is market-based. Thus, the main goal for any business is to be able to meet the standards of consumers for goods and services with regard to QCD. The primary purpose for Kaizen and its activities is to improve QCD. This makes QCD an essential element to ensure the survival of a company.

The value of an item is measured by its quality that is developed by maintaining, sustaining, and enhancing through various methods starting with the purchase of raw materials, to creating, making, manufacturing, distributing or supplying and maintaining the product or service throughout the whole cycle. Imai explained that the process of creating new products and services or developing new engineered ones starts with sketches and documentation. Instead of being discovered in the future the flaws can be easily identified and corrected, which is very expensive to correct if discovered later. To accomplish this management of Japanese companies used quality function Deployment (QFD) or , more commonly called QFD, also known as Quality Assurance Process Diagram, as an instrument.

Cost-efficiency comes after quality, and applies to the total cost of developing, manufacturing products, marketing it to customers, and then delivering the product or service provided by the business. Cutting costs isn't about cost reduction the issue is about controlling costs. The team responsible for managing expenses must oversee the creation, marketing, and selling of high-quality items or services, while maintaining an affordable cost. The manner in which a product or service is created, manufactured and sold will determine whether there is huge resource waste or not. While at the same time increasing efficiency and lowering costs is the most effective option.

Cost management encompasses a broad array of techniques including overall cost control by cutting down on duplication and cost planning to improve the gap between spending and revenue. Cost reduction by removing waste is only possible if the strategies for waste disposal which were previously discussed are properly followed. Reduce costs through changing the structure, engaging in a shrewd negotiation with vendors, or removing employees can disrupt the flow of production, which usually leads to a decrease in quality. Effective management to reduce cost and improve quality also includes other tasks, such as standardization of processes, regulations implementation, training and education. In the present, when teaching employees companies tend to place too much emphasis on teaching techniques. In Kaizen an importance is placed on enhancing the fundamental values of the organization which are continuously enforced by the community via learning as well as teaching programmes. The values that all employees should adhere to within the organisation include discipline, good judgment as well as shared culture and fairness.

Chapter 9: Kaizen's Benefits

Kaizen offers a variety of benefits can be a boon to your business In this article we'll examine the ways in which Kaizen can benefit businesses, individuals and our society.

Motivation

The motivation can be created through showing respect, controlling, or dismissing those who aren't part of the company's fold and also encouraging employees to take those same actions that lead to incremental change and discover solutions to their issues. For example, the company's management recognizes that the morale of their employees is low. To fix this the management then hires employees to solve the problem, which cost more money and cuts into profits of the company. They say they'll increase employee satisfaction and productivity, which also includes breaks at work which eat into the efficiency of the company as well. If the business was able to maintain high levels of morale, employees would have been productive even when they could have a break and saved the business a significant amount of money.

Motivation is crucial and will only happen when you reward employees properly for the work they've accomplished. The most important thing for people is to feel appreciated for the work to do their job. People appreciate little gestures to acknowledge what they've done. People can be unhappy because of issues like recent layoffs, the freezing of pay increasesand the elimination of benefits that they are offered. The majority of employees seem to realize that at any moment the financial challenges of the business are not the fault of the company's management, but rather they are a reflection of the current economic climate. As we've mentioned before, incremental actions are needed to ensure an environment that is sustainable for the business. Morale can be increased by encouraging employees to develop unity by "holding one another" tasks that could be completed for just five minutes every day. It doesn't mean that they need to be physically holding each other but rather acknowledge the hard efforts of everyone to ensure that no one feels you're not part group.

After this and you're ready to go about your day-to-day work. When employees express gratitude to the bosses for being great communication, it's not an indication of their extrovert personality or oratory skills. The reason is that the bosses did what they were required to be doing and made the most of the limited time they had to talk to their employees. They saw their employees as smart people and have a good understanding of what they're doing and spoke to them instead of shouting instructions.

Remember the names of your employees to be able to ask questions directly to them directly. Be sure to are patient and wait for the answers. Also, show gratitude by saying "thank you. It is essential to establish the appropriate emotional tone at the workplace by focusing on small gestures if you wish to maintain good morale. The low morale of your employees is among the most significant corporate issues worldwide however it is easily solved by showing kindness to your employees just for one or two minutes each day.

Communicate with your employees right at the beginning. You will be able to build a great group but they'll never be able to function effectively in a situation where they are not connected to one others. Motivation doesn't originates from the desire to make money in the business world, it originates from our own individual needs. In spite of wanting to make money is linked to your goals or experiences as well as emotions. Your employees are only motivated when they feel connected to you and other people on the team.

It can also assist you in motivating those around you as the leader, as you'll be able to get to know their personalities and requirements. So, you can place them in the appropriate positions and adjust your behaviour to reflect their needs, so they feel a connection to you, and make use of their needs to inspire to push them to work harder. There's no need to hide from the whole thing By establishing connections with your friends, you will be able to engage in more conversations regarding your workers. This will help establish a connection which allows you to understand what's affecting your employees, and also offer them the right guidance to help them discover the motivation to work.

Kaizen can help build motivation by directing the attention of top executives on little tasks such as having a private dialogue with their employees which they often ignore. When all employees are fully embraced by the Kaizen principles, it will become an automatic habit for everyone to acknowledge one another for the tiniest of tasks as everyone will see why these tasks are important to them so much.

Cost Reduction

Kaizen is a Kaizen cost management method is one that demands workers to remove any mechanism that is not a source of effectiveness of the product or service and improvement in quality. It is not in any way that Kaizen hinder the wellbeing of employees within any business. The employees of Kaizen organizations are required to be vigilant about the wasting of capital. If they try to implement methods that undermine the quality of their products or decreases their quality, then the business will remove the technique from its list of permitted and recommended practices. This makes cost management effective and secure.

It may seem counterproductive for employees to manage expenses, but if they are required to take small steps to cut costs for the business, they will be able to manage costs for the business. Employees love being provided with a goal and feel more connected to the business and they will take on the responsibility.

However, it does not allow the management the authority to place the responsibility of cutting costs onto employees and leave them in the lurch. In the first place, it could cause a feeling of anxiety in the employees, which could be harmful for the progress that is taking place. What's required is to change the employees' attitudes toward their work day in the organization, so they can identify opportunities to save money. If you give them the space to think on their own and start to appreciate their inputs and contributions, they'll be the most effective source of information.

As a manager, you need to aid them in conquering the fear that they have of making foolish or stupid suggestions and help them overcome their fear of making judgments. Let your employees think creatively and enjoy their unique thoughts.

Employee-recommendation programs are believed to be reliable in Japan however, the opposite is true for the United States. According to a study in the United States provides cash bonuses which are equivalent to the amount saved by the business as a result of the employee's recommendations. This motivates employees to look for ways to save money, since the cash, in turn, will be put in their pockets.

In contrast to Japan or the United States, the cash rewards are very small or there aren't any incentives whatsoever. Studies on psychology have revealed the complexity of human motivations is. There are two kinds of motivation, both internal and external. The drive that is fundamental to us is derived from our emotions. We are eager to take part in collaboration, be involved in meaningful initiatives, and also feel proud about our work. We want to be assigned assignments that they can rise to and feel proud of the work they are accomplishing. They are driven to create significant things that will can have a positive impact on the world beyond them. External needs are what are in the outside world of a person. Certain of the external qualities can be drivers, like fame and money. External motivations can cause individuals to continue working in jobs that could make them feel stressed. The key to cutting down on expenses is to keep incentives to a minimum. People are more motivated when their needs are satisfied. However, if you simply offer the money, they don't seem to be worrying as much. This is the reason why offering cash rewards as rewards can have a negative impact.

Although some managers attempt to guarantee high-quality results from their employees but they are very rigid in their methods and can cause backlash. Managers who are strict make their employees work harder cause more damage. Employing such tactics will not lead to things being completed quickly and effectively as you'd prefer but it will cause the employee to feel ashamed and uneasy at your presence. They'll be so afraid of you that they'll provide ambiguous answers and will not respond to your questions with confidence. A typical one that is a source of anxiety for all employees includes: "how can the company reduce costs and generate millions of dollars in profit?" This type of question can make the mind of the most intelligent manager and make all employees completely silent. What you should do is use a gentle approach and ask "Do you think your company could save a little small amount of money here or there?" The employee should be pushed to think about issues that they aren't sure ought to be considered when working. Kaizen offers you a myriad of options to implement change among them encouraging employees to think about their thoughts.

It is also possible to put up notice boards on which people can post their ideas. Be sure that these boards are cleared every day and that you take the time to take the time to read every suggestion because it will show employees that their opinions are heard.

Employees are also reluctant to give suggestions since they don't want to cause people mad. They keep any ideas for cost-saving they may have in their heads only when their opinions are very focused on and they're encouraged talk about it. After Kaizen is in place, workers will be assigned the task of identifying ways to cut costs. However, this doesn't mean that you're not in charge as a supervisor and will not be allowed to take any action. What you're responsible for is looking over suggestions that were previously provided and determining the effectiveness of them. You should set up suggestion-management procedures so that this task can be standardized. Consider every suggestion with seriousness when sorting out the suggestions provided.

Keep in mind that some suggestions may seem naive If you look past that, you may discover a brilliant idea. Even the most inexperienced idea could be the key to innovation. Do not forget to thank those who made suggestions that led to the desired change within your company.

Better Accountability

It is important to improve your ability to recognize small errors. Initially, these errors might seem a bit irritating and insignificant If they're not dealt with early enough they can become issues of quality control. Kaizen requires us to spot and rectify mistakes while they're still minor. It is tempting to overlook these issues until they become a disaster. Many businesses prefer to overlook minor mistakes so long as their organization presents itself in a spectacular manner each day.

If a business is successful and continues to be successful, it will continue to respect the elements that have led to its success. These are the employees and administration procedures. If something isn't working properly within a business it's difficult to expose the issue. Most people ignore the mistakes and as a result they miss the chance to improve and to compete successfully. When you ask your employees whether there are any issues that require attention when they reply that they don't have any, take their statement as an indication of red flags. The belief that people will make mistakes is an essential assumption in Kaizen.

Remember that every individual is accountable for the company. Therefore, don't avoid accountability, and encourage your employees to be accountable. Find out how to identify the little errors, state that you would like everyone in the company to be aware of these mistakes too, and provide them the strategies needed to address these issues. Kaizen believes that the responsibility for efficiency and profit rests on everyone within the company regardless of what degree they work at. The management must also allow for easy suggestions and feedback to move from lower employees to the highest-level executives.

Innovation

It is a popular belief that the small actions that we do under the guise of Kaizen produce tiny results. Actually, the small actions will lead to huge innovations that transform the world in a short period of time. Innovation is created through creativity when we begin paying at the tiny moments of life which otherwise seem trivial. Business creativity begins with being curious because, by asking what's missing and what could be wrong, we can make the connection between reality and our imagination. The ability to imagine can lead to successful programs, and the development of new products and improvements. While innovation can be exercised anytime but there are certain times that it really shines through and have an impact. These instances occur when work is being completed but it's only after we've committed ourselves to our work that we will also discover the enthralling potential imagination offers us to improve it. Other examples of innovation include:

* The wastefulness of something: If it isn't in order or time is wasted, or something breaks the equilibrium is lost and this could cause us change our schedules or fix the item that is damaged. Be alert when you encounter these situations because where there is waste there is the possibility for the possibility of change.

* Shame: Sometimes it's the shame that spurs the desire to know more because of an inconsistency between what's been

accomplished and what ought to be done. It's a difficult one, no doubt and the instinct is to attempt to avoid feeling it. This is done by trying to hide the mistakes from others who may not have realized the mistake yet. Some people will admit to their mistakes, and even laugh at the mistake that they committed them, but continue to live their lives as swiftly as they can. When that happens the ingenuity may come in the form of trying to conceal the mistakes.

What you will be able to see is that imagination does not require any special talent. It's all it takes is to pay attention to the things we're doing. It is important to practice discipline to remain focused and inquisitive. The steps of Kaizen can help you maintain your focus and provide the energy you require. Another Kaizen technique is to pay attention to any mistakes that are made if you are looking to increase your imagination. It's a paradox that mistakes must be made because creativity is only triggered through a trial-and-error method, yet simultaneously no one wants to commit mistakes. So, the most effective way to tackle this issue is to create small pilot projects. This is also a way to encourage mistakes that facilitate learning, while at while reducing costs. If you are able to enjoy the benefits of creativity, you'll be able to remember the persistence which paved the way for such creative thinking. Thus patience is a crucial source of long-term advantages.

Better Sales

Sales can be scary no matter how hard you attempt to comprehend it. Sales are a method of manipulation that allows other individuals to exchange cash for goods and services with the intention of obtaining to support the company's plans. Salespeople's role is to market the products and services they're required to sell for money, and also to sell their own company and themselves. However, often, they don't appear as generous to the general public. A lot of people respond to them with anger and disdain, but the salesperson is forced to continue pushing until the job is done and that means what they're required to sell gets sold.

Many are terrified by the idea of making calls to make sales for fear of being apprehensive, and for those there's Kaizen. Many salespeople aren't comfortable with the idea of being scared in their minds when they think of the rate of turnover they are required to reach. Kaizen is an excellent tool to recruit and train sales employees. Kaizen is an excellent tool particularly for frightening scenarios. Many of us have been taught to close our eyes when we are in stressful situations. That doesn't mean that any salesperson a bad one. It's just a natural reaction that one cannot aid. In the beginning, the amygdala of the brain detects an underlying danger to our existence when faced with obstacles that seem to be extreme.

It's better to select salesmen who's brains naturally appreciate the excitement of sales, however they are likely to quit quickly and effortlessly. Training can be extremely expensive for a salesperson. Furthermore, the failure to complete training is not reliable and extremely expensive as well. The question to be addressed is why the majority of management firms don't offer Kaizen methods to manage anxiety and stress within their sales departments. The technique of managing fear is an effective Kaizen method of pushing through the anxiety to think , while paying attention to one thing at each time. Instead of requiring the employees to alter their ways of thinking, you can empower them to make small changes to the way they think.

By taking small steps towards your principal goal can keep your mind relaxed and motivate you to keep moving. Sometimes, a task can be intimidating or terrifying or overwhelming. You may also be feeling stressed emotionally when it appears that it's hard to make the necessary steps. If this is the case how can you proceed? This is where sculpting the mind is required. One of the primary Kaizen tools is mind-sculpting. It's a method of eliminating the psychological resistance that everyone has. Mind-sculpting is a result of a technique called directed imagery. The idea was to aid patients learn a certain physical ability, without actually doing the task. For example when a patient wishes to increase their vocal range and is unable to do so, they must close their eyes and exhale deeply. When they were in a state of relaxation the psychologist will then ask the patient to imagine being in a dark theatre with a calm and peaceful posture before an empty screen. At this point the patient will be expected to be able to hear a voice speaking an example in front of the monitor.

Mind sculpture is a method of drawing upon the lessons that psychologists of other disciplines are learning from the process that guided imagery. It's a fictitious sensory experience that is an entire one. Instead of pretending you are in a theater you can imagine you're doing whatever task. If you're a salesperson, then you can simply imagine the sales call every time. Athletes utilized this type of mental model to train after injuries render it difficult for them to train. After returning to their sport the results are better than ever. Musicians utilize mind modeling, as well. It's a method to train the brain to imagine various scenarios and then teaching it to respond.

For instance, if you are prone to reacting to your anxiety by speaking too fast or withdrawing emotionally, place yourself to be in an emotional sales scenario. Imagine that you are addressing the issue in a manner that you can't do in actual life. Imagine that your entire body is able to let the stress go. Slowly, you'll begin to bring the other person in this scenario real. Think about asking questions that are relevant, addressing the customer's expectations and attempting to understand the needs of their customers with genuine concern. It is important to gradually build your voice more confident and clear.

Do these mind-sculpting exercises for 30 seconds or less each day. If the time you spend every day doing these activities begins to feel effortless and routine, increase the amount of time you devote to practicing. The speed of improvement in the practice of mind sculpting is determined by how much you love the workout. Do not extend the time until the entire exercise begins to appear effortless.

Spend more time on mind-sculpting continuously until you've reached one of two results. The first thing to do is set the foundation for your improvements. You must feel relaxed during the session. You should be ready to perform the exercise even if you prefer to do it one small step at one time. You might also need someone to work with on sales at least a person who you feel comfortable with. If you are looking to challenge yourself, then choose someone who you are scared by. The other chance is that with little or no effort the brain will get better at this task and will even develop new patterns you may not have practiced. It could be that you're on the middle of a sales meeting and suddenly, fresh phrases may pop up in your mind which you never even thought of.

In the end, you'll know the moment when your mind-sculpting was flawless when you're in a difficult selling situation and you can see yourself speaking with the same ease as you've been working on. You'll know you've learned to sell when your discomfort caused you to feel and forget your words becomes a matter of habit and something that seemed impossible to achieve would now be commonplace to you.

If you can just practice just a few minutes per day, or perhaps just a few minutes, mind-sculpting can be extremely beneficial in developing new habits. It's the brain that uses repetition to store the new capabilities within the neurons and the cells. This is the reason why advertisements are continually repeated throughout the day since advertisers understand that this is the only way to reach your brain.

Healthy Workers

At the time no one would have imagined that business leaders would be they were accountable for their employees in good health. However, they do since health insurance has become an expense for business. Employers have been required to protect their workers are protected against health hazards. This is advantageous for companies since if employees keep being sick and unable to attend work, it's going cost the company lots of money. A person who is healthy is one who saves costs for the business by making sure that the work they perform and the pace of production is consistent. The companies are so concerned about the health of their employees nowadays that they organize events like marathons that demonstrate how important being fit is. The company isn't just concerned about the ability of you to go into work. It is also interested in the activities you're engaging in outside of work, what is your diet and whether you're taking treatment of yourself. The majority of companies understand that their employees are valuable resources and they are not readily replaceable. It costs less money for companies to keep the health of an effective worker than hiring a replacement worker in the event of illness.

Many businesses try to improve fitness levels of employees by rewarding them to lose weight. They reward their employees by creating competition among departments, where the department that sheds most pounds, is awarded an extra day of rest. These rewards may be effective in the short-term however, in the long run they don't work because employees will return to their normal routines after the program has ended. The thing managers must be aware of it that losing weight can be the most difficult thing one to do because it requires a total overhaul of the way of life they've built. This means changing how they think, taking care of their health, and having the motivation to improve their performance. This type of self-control isn't easy to achieve Why is that this?

The primary reason is the fear. Kaizen is a belief that changes are scary for people because they have established methods, and people enjoy being organized. A lot of changes can end up feeling anxious. Kaizen can be effective in these circumstances because it breaks the complex change into small step-by-steps, the fear element that comes with a lifestyle change disappears. After fear has gone away and people begin to be more clear-headed and more able to recognize the benefits that come from an improved lifestyle.

How do you educate the employees of your company that Kaizen can be effective in solving their health problems? The only thing you need to do is to explain to your employees the significance of incorporating Kaizen in their daily life. When you break down every task into smaller pieces the whole process will appear more manageable. Kaizen is a way of life and it's not only about business. Once you have accepted Kaizen as an approach to life, you'll start seeing the world from a different perspective. This is the reason Kaizen when introduced into the workplace is a complete source of benefits you would never have imagined. The amount that you put into keeping your employees healthy workforce will be decreased as employees be healthier and lead to less health problems. Kaizen is a sweeping concept and influences all aspects of the company.

Chapter 10: Kaizen And Startups

If you are starting a new venture you'll have plenty of options for introducing Kaizen to gain a competitive advantage from the beginning once you know the basics of the theory. Every leader of a startup dreams of achieving a huge success by selling his product or services. It is not easy for everyone to see their goals by. There is only one out of three thousand entrepreneurs who can get their hands on the keys to success and progress so their business will grow exponentially. This isn't the result of luck or fate. It's the result of carefully crafted decisions and creating an environment that continually expands and develops! It only happens when there is a good educational and developmental environment.

Startups must ensure that their employees are ready to handle any shifts, issues and breakthroughs to be able to take ahead of other businesses. It is crucial to educate the current employees so that they as a result, can educate new employees who could join. In every business, an environment of learning brings the possibility of change, and constant improvement as well as advancement.

This is how you can creating an environment in which innovations as well as feedback and ideas can be discussed openly. Everyone will feel an employee stakeholder of the company as they're an integral part of the process and decision-making is shared by all employees. Encourage your employees to not just follow instructions, but more importantly to make judgments in order for your company to develop into an institution that is able to be competitive with other businesses.

Applying Kaizen

If you are looking to implement Kaizen to your business then these are the areas and concepts that you need to concentrate on:

Establishing an Team

The creation of strong teams is at the foundation of Japanese Kaizen principle, which we have discussed in the previous chapter. According to tradition of the Kaizen practice, the Kaizen team includes experts as well as people who are open to challenging the authority positions. If you're looking to advocate for significant and systematic change that are meaningful, you must see change in the status that is in place. Kaizen's ethos is not to remain in the status of the game. Continuous improvement and transformation are essential to implement the Kaizen principle efficiently.

Enhancement

What can an entrepreneurial setting develop or achieve quality improvement? Start by creating, brainstorming, setting up an open-door policy to feedback, establishing an organizational structure that is less hierarchical and more. Data gathering is the first step into the equation. Begin from the beginning by collecting data about your business. Make use of this information to identify the things that work and don't benefit the business. Even if you decide to drop systems that have been not working from the beginning with regards to new businesses, it can be a bit risky as you don't have all the information you need as the system isn't functioning for a long time. A collection of data over a period of time will allow you to make a more reliable decision and eliminate systems that fail in the course of time. You might not have comprehensive records as a businessman or founder of a business. They are nevertheless essential to long-term decision-making as well as the decommissioning of failed programs. Gather data, analyze it, and determine the necessary adjustments to be made to allow the company to succeed over the long haul.

Implementing Changes

The biggest obstacle to advancement is that it is difficult for companies to re-design the processes, strategies and structures to be able to adjust to new, less expensive and more effective methods of operation. Analyze the impact of these changes on growth for the business. Begin by measuring the effects on the company over a period of one month. After that, analyze the effect of procedural, administrative or other enhancements over a year to make sure that the changes have been successful. This will aid in imagining what the organization will look like, and serve as a crucial to be a guiding principle.

Kontextualizing Kaizen for Startup Culture

Kaizen is about teamwork. It is a central concept and that means you have to incorporate all of your employees completely within the rules and regulations. They must be able to express their opinions as well as logical deductions, insight and business-related feedback as like they are their own. The suggestions and ideas will improve business processes, increasing the effectiveness of the work, reducing money, and improving the criteria used to assess the safety and quality.

Employees must be given the energy to be engaged in their ideas and thoughts and be able to comprehend them. Startups lack the resources required to hire someone who is an expert in Kaizen. By holding Kaizen workshops, you will be able to solve this issue by understanding the best features of this Japanese revolutionary idea and then using it to reach your goals as a manager and in business. Employees are motivated to obtain an assessment in six-sigma business techniques. Other methods of training you can encourage such as project management. This can aid in improving the overall efficiency of employees by reducing errors and improving the structures of manufacturing processes.

Tips and Tips and

Kaizen is more than just making sure that employees are involved in the growth and change process. Here are some Kaizen's theories and tips that will show you how you should do and what to avoid when using it in your business:

1. Don't rely on your expertise alone or be too confident in your abilities over and above the skill of other people. If you are looking to build an efficient and successful enterprise, look for the strengths and insights, expertise and wisdom of others in your team. The strictness of your procedures and structures will hinder your progress while allowing competitors to further improve the field.

2. Don't expect the perfect moment to occur suddenly. With a mere forty percent chance, you could revamp a business and keep developing and improve as you go. If you hold off until everything is in place it will be forced into a state of stagnation.

3. Don't ignore the issues and issues. Take action when you are aware about them, instead of just ignoring them or waiting for the perfect time to address them. The most

effective time to learn is to be on the move. If you don't pay attention to your startup's small, day to day, recurring issues more severe they grow into major issues that cause harm to your startup's efficiency, profitability and growth.

4. When it comes to telling others about something that you aren't sure about and seeking assistance, don't be afraid to ask for help. Don't encourage confusion or confusion to grow simply because it's not clear to you. When you first start, particularly it is essential to debate and discuss instead of allowing confusion to take hold and create a misinterpretation of procedures, processes, and the technologies that will be created in the course of time.

5. The biggest mistakes that startups commit is not basing their decisions on facts and figures , but instead accepting opinions. Everyone wants to offer their opinion since it's a brand new business. It's not a great approach, however in terms of productivity and efficiency. Accept any suggestions or proposals however you can. But, make sure that they are supported by facts whenever you can get them. Remember that decision-

making is not done in a conference room over coffee. This implies that the majority of decision-making is comprised of just thirty percent debate and seventy percent instinctively made decisions happen throughout the day.

6. Never believe that you have everything in order, and you'll need to make changes. It is essential to strive to achieve high-quality growth, transformation, and improvement. This is especially true for an early stage startup, where many structures both operational and organizational and operational, are continually being tested to determine and evaluate what is the best option for the whole company.

How to Implement Kaizen Changes

Begin the Kaizen process by deciphering what aspects of your business are crucial.

While traditionally, Kaizen methods are related to manufacturing and production industry, they are also used in the same way as Six Sigma -- it is now utilized across all business and other sectors. Find out the procedures that could be utilized regularly or weekly and even monthly to help your business start. This will allow you in enhancing the process. It is crucial to have cash reserves prepared to handle and improve the flow of cash. Take care of cash shortages that are urgent by having a credit card for the company as well as other credit lines available. If the processes are not yet implemented (which occurs with the majority of new businesses) It is the perfect moment to create documents that are able to guide the entire business. Don't depend solely on one person's expertise and knowledge. The most common mistake startups make is to depend heavily on their founders' expertise and do not have properly tracing their documentation. In the event that an issue arises, employees should seek out the knowledge of the founder instead of researching what they should do within a logical procedural guide. This isn't a healthy method to implement Kaizen. The most successful Kaizen practice involves keeping track of all consistency processes and giving everyone an opportunity to go over processes whenever they'd like to. This is how you'll be able to develop better results and more efficient procedures. There are some old methods that could be eliminated or modified and result in massive savings.

Which are the key areas that drive or push the organization forward, and are essential to the company's success? Implement our regular training and assessments and make use of the feedback to make improvements. When you record your procedures can be easier to pinpoint ways to improve these by spotting any issues.

Your business will grow eventually and the business climate is likely to change dramatically as the company grows. You'll need to adapt to these changes and adapt to the new rules and regulations. This is essential to the success of your business.

Take a look at these points to incorporate Kaizen in your business What exactly are you're doing? What can you do to make it better? Can you make changes to your current practices in the present even if it's just a minor modification? Maybe change the way you handle your invoices to the point that instead of taking a few hours each day juggling them, you can manage all of them on a weekend or a Sunday to speed up the invoice payment process. There are a myriad of questions you could consider, and will help you find the right way to go when using the Kaizen principle to improve your company's efficiency.

Inspire the Workforce to make steady changes

Does your company provide a healthy and comfortable place to work in that encourages employees to share their ideas and useful suggestions? If this isn't the situation, then you is in need of the Kaizen solution. In a startup, encouraging enthusiasm and generating ideas from employees is more important. It will help employees feel a part of the company's beginnings and boost overall engagement, which could result in an increase in ethical behavior among your employees. Imagine it this way, whenever an employee is permitted to make suggestions in your company's newly-launched business and then their suggestion is taken into consideration, they feel valued as well as respected which encourages them to develop new ideas for improvement and improvement. Give employees the liberty to solve or resolve problems they encounter. The ideal situation is that a supervisor or someone else with similar skills is in charge of the operations and decision-making in the organization. They must, therefore, be able to solve problems and create procedures to accomplish their work more efficient. These procedures will be communicated to the team after they have been established.

However, it is important for employees to believe that they can enhance their work wherever they face difficulties. Inspire and encourage the employees to think of creative imaginative, inventive, and innovative ways to improve their work procedures and tasks. Find opportunities to think differently, and then share them with other employees. Begin to celebrate small victories to create a continuous and continuous improvement community. Every employee in your business must be encouraged to take decisions and take an active part in the process of making decisions. This is particularly important for small companies since you're in a position that the place of each employee is crucial.

They all are part of the early or founding team and feel that they are an integral part of the company's growth of the company's culture, its story, and even its history of the company. They can be more aware of their place in the organization by encouraging these crucial employees to make choices. It's not uncommon for one person to be the whole organization's representative in a small business or a startup and that's why clear communication is essential.

When an employee talks to you, consider their advice, comments and carefully examine what they have to say. They may give you an insider's opinions on something your eyes might have missed. Your employees are those who perform hands-on tasks on various programs and procedures, and they also learn more. Instruct them to investigate the things that work and what isn't. Know that they are specialists in their own processes, and they must be attentive to the ways in which these processes work. This is the reason they are a good choice, and why you should be pursuing them to learn from their experience.

When you implement the Kaizen principle in your business you'll realize that no piece of information is too large or small. All of it is essential and is meaningful. Any opportunity to demonstrate even the tiniest glimpse of progress must be cherished. Small tweaks will result in points that will eventually transform into major improvement over time. This applies to all areas of business, not just the expenditures. There are many ways to waste. various ways. Anything that consumes the time of employees or even the storage space, both virtual and physical space must be investigated and analyzed as a possible area of implementation for Kaizen.

Be aware that the final outcome of your journey isn't progress or improvement. This isn't the end line, but rather an understanding that you must keep track of the discoveries and the progress following the discovery. Kaizen is not about going to a destination but rather moving forward and never ever stopping. It is a process of progress that takes place gradually by taking one step at each step. Development and continuous learning methods are essential to be integrated into the organizational structure of the company and are a part of the fundamental business culture. Do not limit the use of Kaizen to only specific methods or certain occasions only. Kaizen should incorporate into the business culture as an everyday way of living.

Achieving a Win-Win Mentality

If you've worked in the past by the "no" culture business or in a workplace that tells you it's not feasible even though you're aware that it is, it could cause you to feel discouraged. You could have employed a novel and revolutionary method, program or technique only to find out that you couldn't utilize it. Would you like to promote an environment that is toxic in your brand new venture? If you'd like your company to flourish and be successful in the long-term take away the "no" mindset. Learn to teach your employees to use the word "yes" in order to think that it's feasible. From accepting new ideas to helping companies expand and thrive over time All of it can be accomplished by having the right mindset. The "yes" philosophy is bullt on the notion of developing the ability to modify, develop, and help others to work together.

Pareto Principle

To dramatically improve your performance, implement to apply the Pareto Principle or the 80/20 rule. Making small steps to get the highest level of results is the main aspect of this method. Start-up and small-scale business owners must motivate their employees to find major wins for the business and where the business has to work the least and at the same time making the most. This doesn't mean you should ignore the small aspects, however. Be aware that this information can help you or hurt it. The entire spectrum of industries from manufacturing to software design and those who work in the service industry could greatly benefit from making small changes or correcting minor aspects. For instance, a minor improvement in manufacturing processes can transform the reduction in waste by 5 percent to a reduction of 5 percent in the price of the input. The 5 percent savings will increase to an immense amount over the course of.

Constant Change

In other organizations, improvements are made only at certain times throughout the year. Don't let your business adopt a similar pattern that is, where upgrades and updates are only available at certain dates in the course of the year. It is not a good idea to limit updates to a limited number of occasions throughout the year or for general gatherings. Program enhancements and updates to processes are required to be carried out regularly and without interruption. Include it in the daily culture of the company. Create your business from the beginning into an enterprise that is driven by the power of change.

Your employees will be content to show up to work each day when they are aware that they can do something different. They will be inspired by the goals of development as well as the principles and ideologies to make improvements within the organization continuously. Employees will be content to go to work each day when they have discovered an efficient way to work and are confident that they can choose to follow this method to do things. They should be able to celebrate little victories and be given the flexibility to take decisions in accordance with what they believe is the best for overall improvement of quality efficiency, and competitiveness of the business.

Even the least creative employee will often surprise you with their innovative ideas that could boost your business's overall revenue and decrease your expenses. This is a win-win-win for every business when it happens, and that is precisely the purpose of Kaizen is about. Kaizen is about easy solutions. This simple but innovative Japanese method does not have a magic bullet that can solve problems or make obstacles disappear in a single shot. Since Kaizen is "change to improve," its simplicity makes it distinctive since, even though it may be an improvement of a minimal degree but it's about constant improvements. Each change is followed by another and, eventually the entire system gets changed.

Everyone enjoys stories about rapid and radical changes that produce instant outcomes. An easier and more efficient method is the improvement of your personal and organizational performance by taking a few small step-by-step steps.

The way that it operates on a mental level is that radical modifications trigger the mechanisms of anxiety and resistance in our brains, which shuts out our capacity to reason clearly and think creatively. Simpler and less streamlined actions however will not cause us to feel nervous, anxious and anxious. They do not activate the reflexive or warning mechanisms in our brain. Our creative, rational and cognitive processes function effortlessly when there's the gradual and constant change that is lasting and efficient way. This is the reason why we remain convinced that slow and steady can work.

In the same way, repetition helps the process of transforming behaviors into routines and creates a lifestyle. Doing little tasks provides the mind with an immense sense of satisfaction. Continue to make small and improvement to your systems and processes instead of creating radical changes that might cause you to be scared. The emotional blindfolds come off when you make small , gradual changes, in contrast to making large changes that can cause stress in the workplace to overwhelm you and stop you from embracing changes with all your heart. Change can even overwhelm those who think they're not afraid of anything.

Chapter 11: Ikigai

Ikigai is a blend between the two words "iki' which means 'life and 'kai which means 'product' or value.' The idea for ikigai refers to the fact that there exists something that is beyond your existence, or could eventually be a an integral part of your life and give the meaning to all around you, including yourself, your family, friends, reside with, the places you reside, and your surroundings. This is the reason you exist in life as your Ikigai. Being a person with a clear and defined purpose is like knowing what you should do and where you should be and how to operate in all aspects of your life. It's about removing those questions that make you think about every aspect of your life.

Finding your ikigai will make your life easier and more organized since you have a reason to be. When you're in good moods it can provide something you desire more than any other thing, something that will assist you in getting through the rough moments and give you an euphoria towards the close of your day. This will allow you sleep peacefully on your bed in the evening. You'll be able to start your day without having any unneeded concerns about your existence weighing you down.

A lot of people today discover their Ikigai through mistake. They eventually become parents, securing an ideal job, begin traveling, writing a novel in confidence or inventing an idea and then suddenly realize that it was exactly the thing they've were always hoping to accomplish. They realize that this is what their life's journey was meant to be about and they're going to die and live in this way. It will be their gift to the world as well as their commitment to all of humanity and their the reason for their existence.

Many people today are taught this early Many doctors and teachers know this. They were drawn to teaching others or helping people even though they were not old enough to comprehend how they could be in these jobs. For them, it's something that is a calling, or a greater motive, not simply an occupation. This is an intrinsic motivator, and you're aware of the potential to be extraordinary, such as making it into an artist. It could happen at random occasionally.

In some cases, the realization is the result of several years of soul searching however, for many who have been on endless wandering, nothing changes. A majority of people don't find their own Ikigai until older than 40 or so or if they even bother to look. This can lead to errors, such as when you decide to start an organization that you don't really feel connected to, which could cause you to feel a deep regret. A lot of people don't discover their own Ikigai, and struggle to find meaning in their lives. They are left feeling down, and realize that they're just wasting their time. The feeling of being disengaged from your purpose in life causes you to feel that your the life you live isn't worth living.

Let's consider the case of Okinawa to appreciate the significance of Ikigai. Okinawa is a small island located to the south-west of Japan is home to a massive and large population. Okinawa is located in the famous Blue Zone. The inhabitants here live longer than the traditional Western life expectancies. Okinawans are driven by an inner passion to be a part of an intimate community. Ikigai is the reason why their lives are extraordinary.

If life were as simple it was that easy, we'd all likely to last for more than ninety years. The world instead is filled with a myriad of illnesses related to food, chemicals emissions, lifestyle and. We're too busy to consume the foods we need and are too busy with our jobs to engage in routine workouts. There's not enough time for developing friendships or establish close social bonds. A lot of contemporary cultures in the West are based on achievements which can be measured in money and fame. Okinawa is different . It is the only place on earth where people lead better and live longer than nearly everywhere in the world. People on Okinawa claim that the secret to survival lies in harnessing the power of purposeful energy and removing negative ones. They lead a happy, long and purposeful existence.

The term "purposeful" is an important word to highlight. Even people who are retired get up each day with a sense of direction and a goal to reach for the day, regardless of how tiny it might be. Despite the island's remote and harsh environment, as well as its restricted access to modern medical and health treatment, Okinawans are fitter than their Western counterparts. They're not suffering from the cardiovascular disease, cancer as well as diabetes or psychological problems like dementia or depression.

People in Okinawa devote their time to creating meaningful and personal relationships with one another. Within a particular time frame family and friends support one another, and nobody is alone and uncared for. The elderly serve the younger and the young help the older and both in a relationship that is positive and warm. These social networks can help ease anxiety, while also offering security and safety in daily life, as people realize that they have others who can count on them if they're in any sort of need. The majority of Okinawans are slim healthy, light, and healthy diet that is mostly based on vegetables as well as tofu. They eat healthy, low-carb meals along with various soy-based foods. The diet allows them to lead a an enlightened lifestyle.

Alongside sugar, fats and foods that are highly processed Eliminating meat can help in fighting heart disease and weight gain. Green tea that cuts fat is an integral element of the diet. They are awash with ginger, mugwort and an assortment of herbs and chilies too. Apart from eating healthy as well as sweets, Okinawans are committed to exercising frequently. They build their daily routines around dancing, walking and even gardening. They spend a lot of time in fresh air and enjoy the benefits of the great outdoors and sunshine. They are more secure and have stronger muscles, higher levels of vitamin and generally enjoy more positive moods due to the constant exposure to sunshine and exercise.

Okinawan life isn't a stroll through the forest. Okinawans aren't just walking in the forest. Okinawans have learned to let the past go where it belongs , in the dark and strangled past. Instead, they're focused on the pleasures of the present. What we must learn from this society is that the quality of life shouldn't be measured in terms of fame or riches. Instead, we must strive to enhance excellence in our interactions, feel at peace with everyday actions and live an enjoyable and active lifestyle.

The key to the longevity of the islanders could be traced to a single term: ikigai. This generally refers to your purpose for existence or an inner motivation to get out of your home and perform your work. It can also be described as an intersection of four distinct elements which are what you're attracted to what you're good at, where your talent lies in, the way you earn an income and the things that society requires. The majority of Japanese believe that everyone is a ikigai or destiny. They were made to be with. While some individuals are able to identify their ikigai immediately while others have to discover it over time. It is vital to keep going when you are in the latter category. After all, it's ikigai that eventually inspires you to leave your bed when you're down and depressed.

Okinawans are also excellent at what they do. They possess a high level of accuracy and place an importance on the finer details of their work. For example, a professional craftswoman working in a painting machine in Okinawa is well-known for her brushes since she has spent her entire life working on the art of attaching human hair to brushes. She's been able to complete her job with remarkable ability and precision because she believes that it will be her goal in life. So, if career in ikigai is what you're working engaged in, you'll never be able to retire for in the future. If your ikigai is something that gives you joy and tranquility, don't give up in that area for a long time. Okinawans adhere to these principles and are therefore active later in their lives. When they must retire, they'll be able to find ways to remain involved with their communities by doing things like gardening or doing other work.

Define Ikigai

How do you find the personal ikigai of one's own? The first step is understanding the two meanings of life and the way they affect our lives.

Love

The most basic definition of the universe is love. It is the primary reason that explains why we exist on the planet. Every one of us is searching for it every day regardless of whether it's our parents or our partner. Love comes in many ways, and in a variety of ways, but it can even be harmful. The reason that love is a defining factor in life is because it could become a definition of us. If you're in love with someone and you believe that you'll be willing to offer your life to that person, which gives you an idea of direction. As a man, you might believe that protecting the love that you love is for your existence. However, the issue of this belief is that the love may also be a problem if we aren't sure the true meaning of love.

Love isn't just about people. You shouldn't think you are taking care someone is all that you are being. What happens if the person goes out of your life or doesn't wish to be protected by you for any longer? We've all heard about broken-up stories that go wrong that saw people take extreme measures after losing love in their lives. It happens because the person you were into love with is temporary and not permanent.

What kind of love Ikigai speaks about is love that transcends places and people. It's a feeling of being deeply in love with yourself and realizing that you have the entire universe inside the person you are. It may sound cliché but keep in mind that everything you see exists because you are. It means that the world isn't a part of your mind. Therefore, everything is part of you.

How do you determine what it is that you really enjoy? Try the Marie Kondo method. Look through the items you own and discover those that are meaningful. If you have the car you drive What does it say about you? It's that you're rich? Does that really mean anything? The only way you can discover genuine love for yourself is by looking for things that don't have a direct use but you still keep them. A photo from the past of you with your loved ones, for instance is it helping you by any means? No. Then, why do you feel so in love with it? It is clear that it's the image you really appreciate. It allows you to go back and discover what's important and what's not.

Talent

The second reason to live is the ability. It's not talent in the sense ability to do anything, but rather what you make. Human beings are unable to discern what our purpose in life, since there isn't much around ourselves to explain who we really are. If someone asks what you're like, most people simply reply with their achievements. Why is this? Because we believe that what we've done are more tangible and important than we actually are. Our talents bridge this gap since it reveals what we're good in creating and how it is related to our own nature.

There are some who are great singers and what does that tell us about them? It means they can start with a profession and make money? This is the most common answer. However, those who love singing recognize that singing is a means to express their inner emotions. It's a way of expression that is uniquely the individual. People who draw art are able to express the emotions they are feeling and help to deal with their emotions. It is thought to be therapeutic as it helps us channel our emotions inside.

You may think that you've no talents, but that's likely that you haven't been looking for it. Your talents don't have to be something that is typical like dancing, singing or even painting. There is a lot of joy in any endeavor, whether it's sewing or organizing your home. You'll be able to tell if something is your skill when it's something you just want to do it when you're not having anything to do, but instead feel that you're moving in the right direction. It's like taking away the persona you've been to become one with the work in front of you. In this way, you'll recognize what you are most at home with.

Ikigai and Entrepreneurship

From the very beginning of history, seeking a happy life has been the primary goal of every human being. We seek out things that bring us joy as well as that are outside our home. We all wish to make a difference in the community and to create our world to a manner that is in line with our personal reality. Japanese concept of "ikigai" should not be something you can find outside of the office to keep you from your work and must be part of all aspects of life. We spend the majority of our time at our office, and it could be hard to be comfortable when we must make an epic effort every day to get out of bed and get to an office in which we aren't appreciated. This is that we begin our individual journey to the world. If you don't feel fulfilled, we may feel disengaged. Employees in any company must always be considered a top priority over and above the achievement of personal goals like the pursuit of fame or money. Although this may sound like a childish approach however the fact is that when you take care to look after the well-being of your employees the profits of your business are likely to grow ten times over. From a financial point of view by investing in the motivational aspects of your employees, the ikigai that you create for your entire team will increase your profit.

There is always the concept of fulfillment while considering finding a suitable place to work. However, there are other things to consider also. Here are some of the things you must study to figure out which area you would like to be employed:

* Trust among leaders and colleagues
* Take pride in the work you're doing.
* Workplace comradeship.

Trust is the first location you must begin to grow and develop as it is the glue that holds the entire workforce together. The foundation of trust is the employer-worker relationship. There are many benefits you can enjoy from establishing trust in your office. The office staff will be more relaxed and will all feel like they can count on one others for help, everybody will feel valued and they will be more comfortable discussing their thoughts and ideas.

Camaraderie and pride are among the most significant and becoming less common every day. These values are perceived by each person in a different way as they are based on each individual's character and needs. They are based on the relationship to the person who is working and their job (pride) as well as the relationship with their coworkers (camaraderie). The expectations each person must meet from their job to ensure that they are satisfied are individual and unique and ensuring that everyone is doing the right job to achieve their objectives is essential. How well relationships are built between colleagues is contingent on the personality and preferences of each person and their requirements. Management's ability to connect their personalities effortlessly and to put similar individuals in the same department is essential for camaraderie to take place.

The camaraderie and pride can be connected to ikigai when you consider the concept of 'living and living and letting live taking into account. Recognizing the importance of others in life, while respecting your own is a recipe for an unison working environment even when individuals may clash with one another.

In order to create a business with happy employees, you must address the three factors discussed above: hope enthusiasm and camaraderie. The best method to create an atmosphere that is happy is to listen the employees' personal desires. If you can keep them happy and happy, it will ensure that your company is successful. One thing you must remember is that what people have to say matters more than anything you are able to say. A lot of people believe that leadership is about dominating and taking all the time in conversations and meetings as is possible, but this is not true. As as a leader, it is important to be aware that even if you do work. You're not the only one creating worth for the business All you're doing is overseeing and directing the work of other people. Your role is to listen to what people are saying - listen to other people's opinions whenever they can because it will provide you with more insight into their mental state. This allows you to use this information to assist them to perform better. Your employees should be open about what they're thinking rather than hide the thoughts from you.

If you wish for other people to express their opinions Your first job is making them feel comfortable. Make sure you don't check your phone or laptop constantly getting distracted by other people and the other person needs to feel as though their emotions are welcomed in the space. A good listening skills requires you to get to understand your employees more; you won't be able to know the meaning of someone's words until you know their persona as well as their background and the is their personality. If you are a boss, you must remember to engage to your staff on an even scale, be sure to by sharing some of your own personal information in the same way, and this means that the personal bond that you create will increase the level of empathy. This is also the best method to make people feel more human; if your goal in leading people is to make them feel like herds it is possible to combat this by personalizing individuals. It is essential to view them as people with dreams, families and a life that goes beyond work.

One thing that many managers tend to overlook is that you only inspire employees to be more productive in a way that makes them feel like part as part of your team. If you recognize their efforts and then promote them to higher places, they will begin to feel satisfaction with what they do. Most importantly, the most effective method to create confidence is to allow employees to contribute something that is meaningful. If a worker is passionate about the environment, you should allow them to work in an area that is focused on saving the planet. This will give them a reason that encourages employees to do their best regardless of whether you pay them (although you should). Solidarity in the workplace is making sure that everyone feels as if they are free to express their opinions without hesitation. Even if you're the manager, you need to ensure that your employees feel that you regard them as an integral part of your household. They shouldn't be afraid by you as it will not make them feel that they are part of something however it will discourage them.

Finding your Ikigai

There are some who believe they don't feel the joy of living in their individual abilities or their thoughts. Many people are forced to endure the pressure of getting to get up from mattress and pushing themselves to complete the work. The feeling of passion and energy is now an ephemeral memory for many of us. Many people find it difficult to find the spark of passion when they work, and the notion to find their own ikigai hadn't yet had the chance to emerge.

Based on a study of Igai, one of the principal findings was that extrinsic motivation isn't achievable in various ways encouraging people to buy tangible objects isn't realistic. Researchers have discovered that people are only responding to the inspiration that is intrinsic to them. Japanese philosophy requires that people find their ikigai. When you reflect back, you'll realize when you were a child, you may have displayed an unusual inclination to something. When we reach the age of maturity, what we are will depend on the socio-economic factors that affect us, such as the things we choose to do, how our parents believe we should be doing and what income we believe we need to live up to our ideal standards.

There are four things you should ask yourself to help improving your day-to-day orientation. When we are surrounded by the daily haze it can be difficult to recognize our capabilities. There are four key questions that can assist us in finding the ways. Keep them in a spot in which you frequently encounter them. You can use them to create an compass to guide you closer to the goal. These are the questions:

What's my role in the game which is called life? Do you think you are an extrovert or introvert? Do you think you'll enjoy doing the work with your own or in an organization? If the answer is a combination of both, will you still be happy with the task? Write down the answers to these questions each whenever you encounter the possibility of a place in which you could work and build an environment.

* What is the one thing I feel fulfilled about? What is the time when time seems to fly by? What can you be able to do for hours and not be bored? It could be a task that makes you feel fully engaged and not want to give up.

* What type of work is easy for you? Is there something that you find easy that others appear to be having a hard time? The majority of people today find it easy to organize their documents in a simple manner and others excel in evaluating multiple perspectives. It is essential to discover your strengths and what you're naturally skilled at.

* What was something you truly love doing as in your youth? This question can help create the ikigai's foundation. Did you find the experience in the intrapersonal, psychological moral, physical auditory, linguistic or even visually? This will help you determine what type of experience you're drawn toward.

Ikigai is the intersection point that connects four of the most fundamental elements of our lives such as passion, vocation work, and the everyday. What we all seek is ultimately the spot that is the ideal combination of the four components. It is a place where everything you are passionate about meets what you excel at, is a reflection of the things you are most proud of within yourself and has a deeper significance that connects you to the world. Ikigai is only complete if the reason you choose to use it is something of a community service. This is because we prefer to give gifts rather than receiving them. Once you've defined these components then the next step is to begin working on your compass. Work on your queries, and then see if you can find something that is suited to your answers.

Chapter 12: Additional Uses Of Kaizen

Kaizen isn't an only business rule and is applicable to almost every aspect of your life. This chapter we'll try examine the ways in which Kaizen as a concept can aid you in different areas of your life.

Personal Development

Beyond Kaizen's corporate method, there are more aspects of Kaizen beyond what is used in the business world. Everyone is believed to be driven to improve themselves in one way or other. Kaizen gives the training employees require for personal growth by introducing different concepts and techniques. It assists them in evaluating their lives against the established standards of their physical, social, emotional and psychological well-being and, when feasible, make suggestions to improve their lives. A lot of people who participate in this process prefer to concentrate on strategies that take small actions that help them live their lives more easily.

When someone begins to engage in Kaizen methods, the majority of the things they'd like for improvement are of a physical nature, such as sleeping, exercise and eating habits. If the new behavior is successfully followed, they are encouraged to move on towards the self-improvement level which is where their emotional aspects are put into focus. Anyone who participates to Kaizen will notice that the Kaizen initiatives will see an improvement in their behaviour and, with each day, they will be happier. They will be able to improve their exercise practices, eating habits and even their sleep. Additionally, they will begin to display more complex behaviors in relation to their interpersonal skills and even their spiritual commitments. They'll also be capable of establishing the Kaizen attitude in their own lives, and will greatly benefit from this in every aspect of their lives.

The term "transition" is believed to be an ongoing process. If one is successful in a specific area of their life, he or is motivated to apply similar methods to the other aspects of their lives. The concept of Kaizen allows people to make changes through setting small- and long-term and mid-term goals, and to contemplate making small changes in the process of achieving the goals. The requirement to be successful in more areas than one is not over when Kaizen is implemented. This is the reason why acceptance of the Kaizen theory of continuous advancement is promoted. It is important to keep in mind when trying to alter your behavior and habits that not all practices cause harm or have negative consequences for your health. The way you live your life is not always negative but it's the way we interact with them that make them to be. They are required for us to to perform our daily tasks in a certain way. Negative feelings can be transformed into positive ones, and can be utilized to help us feel tired and stressed. They can help keep us secure and to help us. The idea of leaving our routines' security zone can be a challenge which is why we would rather carry on our daily lives as if we're some kind of robot.

You may be wondering the reason why it is difficult to change habits. Did you be aware that repetitive behaviours save us from hours and effort? It's scary and daunting when it comes to changing them as they are sedatives and reduce stress by creating familiarity. In order to make change in routines it is first necessary to understand the process by which we were first influenced into this behaviour. The next step to address is to change the patterns and identify the causes that lead to undesirable behavior. Apart from knowing the triggers that lead to these behaviors, you need to be aware of the rewards that we typically receive through this actions. Think about how these incentives influence our future actions as we want to repeat the same rewards in the future. Also, consider how these behaviors can bring lasting rewards should they be altered.

The next question you'll likely be asking is what time does this process take? The time required for an individual to attain automated processing varies from individual to the next. It is dependent on the person as well as the context they've been raised in, as well as the attitude of the individual toward changing. To change behavior you must be able to master the new behavior continuously expanding the link between the context of the person and the particular habit that is being practiced. The more often a pattern is repeated, the more likely it will be instilled.

Dietary Habits

Implementing Kaizen techniques to improve your food habits could be beneficial to people who wish to change their eating habits. Instead of limiting or eliminating the pleasure of eating, look to make small changes to your eating habits and food in order to develop an enlightened mindset that will improve your body and mind. Let's examine the ways Kaizen can transform your eating habits into three distinct objectives: goals in the medium, short and long-term.

Drink More Water

The quantity of water you drink every day is contingent the gender of your partner, the food you consume and the amount of exercise you perform, and your environmental conditions. Incorporating coffee, milk tea, tea, and drinks without sugar into your daily diet and in the same time drinking water is not a problem. A lot of people don't drink water, however since the advent of Kaizen and Kaizen, it's going to become a habit which will benefit your body even if you don't remember to. Be sure to pay attention to your body's needs for water, but keep in mind to drink water every couple of hours. Do not drink too much as it could be harmful to your body.

There are a lot of meat eaters around the world right the present. Reduce the amount consumption of animal products by our body will have many advantages for your overall health. Kaizen is a great method to make this transition since it's a slow method of improvement. All you need to do is slowly shift and eat more fruits and vegetables. In the Japanese diet vegetables play an important part. It's also a less expensive diet that contains all the nutrients your body may require.

Kaizen is a great way of incorporating fruits and veggies to your daily diet. It is important to reduce your intake of sugar when you are vegan. The consumption of soft drinks and sugar can be dangerous and this is accurate to a certain degree. Also, make sure to quit having fizzy drinks. However, this doesn't mean that you have to reduce your sugar intake completely since the fruits you consume when you're continuing your

Kaizen implementation are only natural sugars. Since it's a gradual procedure it is recommended to cut off your sugar intake. that you typically consume, reducing your intake by half and then gradually ease it out. Your body requires an adjustment period to adapt to a different source of energy , such as natural sugars. This is a long some time. Avoid eating cereals as preserved sugar is added in them. These can be detrimental for your body. Also, you should stop adding sugar to hot beverages such as tea or coffee.

Limit the portion of your Diet

This refers to decreasing the amount of food that you consume. We are prone to eating too much since we don't evaluate our food using proper portions. Start by taking a look at the calories of your food using small bowls. After eating and cooking, be sure that there aren't any leftovers, and then monitor your appetite levels.

Eat Carefully

Concentrate on and fully appreciate every bite you take. It is best to have little or no distractions while eating dinner, shut off the TV and avoid eating while sitting in front of your laptop. Focus on the preparation of your meal rather than ordering items from the outside. If we don't take note of our food choices, we feel hungry, because we didn't appreciate the food, and instead we just gulped the food down. Therefore, even if you're full you're still craving food which is what causes overeating.

Mindset

Your personality and mental state can be the most valuable asset or the most significant barrier in the way of your goals. The inner issues we face remain in the shadows of our talents and abilities, regardless of the effort we make to conquer them. This is why we have a difficult time achieving goals, even though we're capable of reaching these goals. The change in your attitude isn't something you can do in one day. You've been influenced by your beliefs or ideals, as well as your behavior throughout your years of training. The bad habits and assumptions were a struggle to blend seamlessly with your personality. However, once you accepted these habits, they began to influence your behavior. Thus, to replace these unhealthy habits and erroneous values with healthy practices and beliefs will require a continuous development in your everyday life. Kaizen is here to assist you in this endeavor.

Learning About Yourself

All of it starts with the initial step of getting to understand yourself. It is essential to implement Kaizen to work on improving your routine and learn more about how you behave by observing your behavior each day. It is important to discover why you're reacting to situations in the way you are reacting to the Internet being slowed down by tension and anger. Also, hopefully you'll learn to manage and control your emotions in the moment.

Reversing your Convictions

Your beliefs will prevent you from making an improvement to your lifestyle. Even if positive changes challenge your beliefs and beliefs, you're not likely to embrace the change to your lifestyle unless you modify your thinking. If you think that yoga isn't effective even if you believe it does, the chances that you'll be using it for exercise and help your body heal are virtually nonexistent. An untrue belief that is in opposition to an action positive blocks the possibility of achieving significant transformation. This kind of challenge blocks the power of Kaizen to alter your life. You can use Kaizen to create small habits slowly However, you can also develop little beliefs gradually. A person who lacks confidence in something through an optimistic conviction could end up creating the habit. If you aren't sure you'll have the endurance to run just seven miles, begin by thinking that you could run for three miles. If you believe this and are able to achieve this amount of physical effort are you sure you'll be able to run for seven miles? Whatever your number do not think that Kaizen can make the unattainable possible. Kaizen will show you that through small steps, anything is possible and achievable, but only if only take each step one at a time. When we witness evidence to support our beliefs, we change our views. If you decide to start practicing yoga and you see benefits then there's no way you're going to ignore its healing potential. Because Kaizen's primary goal is to provide your subconscious mind with little proofs of its effectiveness and bringing about changes at a moderate speed. However, it has the ability to change your character and values for the rest of your life.

Change your patterns

There are certain behaviors which determine our response to events that occur around us. These fixed patterns are brought to action by the changes that occur in our surroundings. There are many positive trends like finding the positive even in negative situations and feeling empowered when things turn bad and a respectful treatment of people regardless of what. Other patterns of behavior can be negative, for instance, being irritated in stressful situations or losing all faith in the process, not focusing on essential tasks, and ignoring connections. In the event of a life-threatening incident someone may be energetic, while the other may be overwhelmed by anxiety. This is why some are seeking adventures in life, and others prefer security. Anyone who wants to live in an environment that is healthy will be difficult to leave their home or country in search of a better job or an improved life.

It's quite a big deal to completely change your status in life and it's also a cause for concern for many. With Kaizen these terrifying situations can be slowed down by breaking them into smaller segments.

Imagine being in something which makes you feel terribly as well as out of your control. Or something that's out of your comfortable zone. Maybe it's elocution, or even skydiving. It doesn't matter which kind of situation it's. We develop our character and resilience by allowing our minds to this kind of anxiety. If you're planning to move to a different city like, say you can prepare yourself to think about your future in the new area. To prepare yourself for the changes, you should also visit the city a number of times. The goal is to stop allowing the brain to think too much about every circumstance. By controlling your fears you can control the reaction you will take. Every situation is so difficult that it is unable to be taken on - it's the response to these situations that defines your character.

The Kaizen approach of gradual changes keeps you from becoming annoyed by things since instead of putting the entire job on your own You just took on only a portion of it. It is best to pick the most stressful part of the situation and work on it first until you feel less anxious. After that, you can move on to another aspect of the circumstance.

Management of Private Time

The management of their personal time is a huge issue for the majority of people. 24-hours a day may not seem like enough time to complete all the tasks that you must complete. However, it's not about how much time you're working, but what's crucial is how you utilize these hours. The ability to manage time is something which every person should develop to enhance their performance at home or at work and to achieve a better quality of life.

It is possible to apply the Kaizen method if you'd like to make more time. Make a list of all the crucial things you'll have to accomplish this week. These tasks may vary from routine tasks for the day to ones that you'll need to finish in order to meet your goals for the long term. Write down the things that you tend to indulge in and then spend your time doing it. This could include things like watching TV or playing video games or simply taking a nap. Naturally, with Kaizen it isn't necessary to eliminate all your annoying behaviors in one go. Instead, you must gradually eliminate one thing from your list of undesirable activities , and then add another on your checklist of beneficial activities. Reduce by 20 minutes of the time you watch TV, and the time you've accrued can be put to use to take a walk of twenty minutes or planning a brainstorming session. The goal is to create time for healthier activities by cutting down the time you spend on unhealthy routines.

Finding the Perfect Self

What's your ideal image of you? Answering this question with reflection will result in an enlightenment process which will help you realize what you value about your own self. Every one of us has in our minds a vision of who we would like to be. Your ideal self may be a regal or humble. It is possible that you will adopt the traits of a famous persona in a film. No matter what it is something that all of us strive to achieve in our lives even though many of us have never been reach it. While the final step towards self-actualization is unattainable you do, the

Kaizen method can offer us a path of living that allows for continuous changes, which brings us closer to the imagined self.

You're focused on a particular area of your life by using Kaizen and you're trying to make it more powerful. In the example above, if you'd like to feel more confident. How do you do doing that? For the majority of people, confidence is just an indication of their current financial situation. But, this kind of metric of confidence can be limiting, because if your account at the bank isn't growing, so is your confidence. Take a different route, then. It's likely that money will remain an extremely volatile element that you live. Why not put your beliefs with something that will remain with you for the rest of your life. It could be that you have a knack in music or are extremely knowledgeable on a particular area, or you're an individual who is the main attraction at a party. Whatever it is that you are gifted with you should learn to see this ability as the main basis of confidence. You can then get rid of the idea in your mind that the size of your bank account is the determining factor in who you are.

Leave the house dressed in your everyday clothes, and with just a little money to try this. Make an effort to meet people and engage in discussions that are free of your financial interests. However, you should inform them immediately that you're having financial difficulties and document the way they respond. You'll find that the general public's perception of you isn't dependent on such superficial matters. If they only value you because of money then you shouldn't be around them at first.

Saving Money

Everyone wants to earn the most money we can. Everyone knows how wealth can be the universal measurement of success. It makes you feel safe, makes you feel secure, and gives our a sense of calm. It's probably the most appealing concept that exists and people are enthralled by it and will take any step to acquire the money. The process of accumulating wealth isn't any shortcuts. When people consider making money, they immediately think of owning a huge home, a car and a massive bank account balance. What Kaizen is teaching people about the value of money is it's in the smallest things that cash can be saved. While it may not appear appealing saving little by small until you've earned a substantial amount but it is actually the most effective method to accumulate wealth.

We aren't aware of that we're wasting many dollars. We don't take note of the amount we spend and the places we spend it. If you pay attention to the little things and focus on incremental improvements, you'll be in a position to make savings a habit. Because Kaizen is about the tiny steps, begin planning what you could accomplish to help save some money during the week and then begin to think about ways to make savings this month. Go through your all your expenses and find the ones which are impacting your account the most. There are several areas to work on:

Credit Cards

Credit cards are fraud and are designed for you to feel wealthy to keep you purchasing things until you realize all the money that you believed you had was fictional. The first thing a financial adviser will advise you is to stop using your credit card since it forces our brains to view money as a commodity , not a laborious resource that's hard to obtain. A majority of people do not have any money at all; people are being in debt and believing that they're wealthy. The most effective method to eliminate debt on your credit cards is through the consolidation of your debt. Get rid of your credit card and convert the remaining credit into a loan can be paid off gradually. Or, you can simply pull on your pants and get going to get rid of the obligations as soon as you can.

Phone

The phones have an aspirational look to them, and every one of us want into the latest technological advancements that everybody is talking about. But, do you really need the latest variant of the phone because it's got the latest options? No. The choice of a less expensive phone may make you feel that your peers will be judging your choices, but it's much better than enduring debt and not eating out all to buy a higher-quality camera. They are also costly because they cost you additional costs. Cut down on your data plan as well as other similar items that you don't actually require.

Food

We all love spending money on food. Even if we're not able to afford a lot amount of cash to spend, it's tough to not spend money on that one meal at your favourite restaurant. The first thing to stop doing is eating out. Even if you have to eat out frequently due to your work or obligations to others, try to limit this as much as possible. Limit yourself to a couple of days in a week that you're permitted to purchase food. Also, get awake early each morning, and cook your own meals that you will require during working time. So, you don't need to visit the canteen or to a restaurant for lunch.

Also, you should consider more efficient grocery shopping. You can buy everything you require to get through the month in large quantities. Find the most affordable supermarket near you, and those that offer the most attractive discounts or offers. These are the simple items that people tend to overlook because they're in a hurry to make a change. It may take another 30 minutes to drive to a supermarket that is less expensive, but it's farther away.

However, at the end the day, it'll cost you less which is why it's worthwhile.

Subscriptions

Today, everyone pays for Netflix, Hulu, and Amazon without considering how much these subscriptions could end costing you in the end. If you are paying monthly charges which you don't consider vital, then you need to eliminate the bills. Do you really have a need for these services? Are there alternatives to alternatives to this subscription? Maybe you could share the cost of the Netflix subscription with a partner or coworker, thereby saving quite a bit of cash by the close of the year.

Electricity

Many of us do not pay attention to the quantity of energy we're spending because it appears like an infinite supply of resources, yet it's actually not. Heating and cooling use up tons of energy. You can cut down your monthly electricity bill by half if recently started closing your heater or air conditioner when you're not using it. Closing power sockets as well as light bulb sockets when not in use can be useful. The fact that a majority of people turn on light bulbs even in direct sunlight they can be in is an enigma. It is essential to think about the tiny choices you make since they could make a huge difference.

It's not necessary to change everything and some of them you may not be able handle. It is important to try anew - each day, you'll find an area where you can possibly save money, and all you need to do is practice the option regularly until it becomes a routine. If you save money make sure you don't waste it spending it on things that aren't worth it or for a home renovation. It is best to start saving your money and invest it to make sure it replicates itself as soon as is possible.

Investment

Being a single parent isn't easy since you're constantly worried about the lack of enough money. The worry of missing a day of work could be extremely stressful, and could eventually cause permanent negative effects on your mental and physical well-being. The best method of getting rid of this fear is to begin saving money to ensure you have a back-up plan. This can give you confidence and can be a huge help to help you overcome the financial burdens. The process of investing is gradual and unlike films, it isn't necessary to search for an amazing stock to become wealthy immediately. All you need to do is choose an efficient and secure financial instrument to place money into slowly. Once you've gotten used to it and you begin to forget that you have this savings; in the end it will be a greater sum you can draw upon in the event of emergency.

It's your decision to decide which kind of instrument you'd like to invest in which could include mutual funds, stocks or even an account for savings. It is important to never invest with the full understanding about what you're investing in. Make sure to speak with an expert in financial planning If that's too costly for you then you could always go to the Internet. Be sure to conduct thorough research prior to deciding to invest any money. Don't waste your money on trying to duplicate the same thing. Start with an amount of money, and once you are sure that your investment is secure you can increase your investment slowly and continue to do the little things.

Making investments with money could put lots of stress on your wallet. The best thing to do is assess the amount of money you've got and what your future expectations are for this money to be steady. This will help you determine whether you're able to put money into investments or not. If you are employed in the field where income fluctuates frequently, it's not a great decision to invest a large amount of cash. If your income increases suddenly in the meantime, you may also increase the amount you invest. You just need to determine your financial situation and basing on that, decide what direction you would like to take forward with your investment. Examine your income each month. For each increase in income, put in 5 percent more. And any time your income decreases do not invest in that month. What Kaizen really requires is to be patient. Be patient in your investment decisions and make small steps , even if they're months apart. This can reduce the risk you're taking , while at the same time increasing the potential for gains. It's also a game that is why you must be alert to areas to invest in.

Health

Learning the Kaizen method can allow you to live a healthy life. You've likely made promises to yourself countless times to eat better and healthier. You've probably desired to be more active and live a more healthy lifestyle without drinking or smoking. However, it seems that there's no way to make it work. Most likely, it's because your goal seems to be too large, and the exercise routine video that lasted two hours you attempted to watch was too much to handle every day. It is a good thing that you are able to build your wellness gradually through Kaizen and not put excessive stress on your body or mind.

Just a little weight loss or lifestyle changes provide a wealth of health advantages. If you take part in moderate workouts every day for only 20 minutes, you'll reduce the likelihood of suffering from health issues like heart disease, diabetes, as well as high cholesterol. Because Kaizen offers a comprehensive method that includes exercise and weight loss, they are inextricably connected to the benefits to your lifestyle that come from Kaizen. If you're looking to shed twenty pounds like the rest of the world. If you aren't working out it could be an overwhelming goal. This is why you should break down the goal into smaller, smaller, and more manageable 2 pound weekly goals. This way, you're taking ten weeks to reach your goal instead of hoping for immediate results. Once you've established your weekly goal it is time to take smaller measures of Kaizen to reach your goal. Here are four steps:

Check your weight daily

This simple routine will help you remind yourself each morning about your weight. Studies show that those who take a look at their weight daily tend to practice healthy eating and exercise more. As a result weight loss becomes easy to attain. This is a good habit to develop to prepare yourself to exercise and eat. It will also motivate you as you begin to exercise routine and diet. It will also provide your brain with a the feeling of satisfaction each when you notice that you weigh less than the previous day. You will be motivated to stick to your fitness and diet plan.

Make a Stand

What number of hours do you spend sitting down? Many people have jobs which require them to sit for between nine and thirteen hours, based on their job and lifestyle. Some people can find enough energy to get out and purchase the standing desk.

Instead, you should get up every 30 minutes or so for just about a minute. Go for a walk around the building or just do a few stretching exercises. After that, you can return to working. Begin to slowly increase the time from 2 minutes to 4 minutes after a certain amount of amount of time. It is best to look for small ways to extend the length of time you're standing particularly for those who are seated a lot at work. It's also the case who spend a significant amount of time playing games or watching television. It is possible to stroll around during commercial breaks on television shows when you spend a lot of your time seated all day. These little changes will make major changes to your life and help you lead a healthier and happier life.

You can take the Stairs

Your office building or your apartment also have the stairs. It is a good idea to keep using the stairs. In the event that your workplace is tall to reach every step, you can make use of half initially. Gradually over the next weeks, you will be adding more staircases. The aim is to increase your daily steps gradually. It's possible to be stunned to see the improvement you've made within a couple of months. the only thing you'll be able to remember is how tired you felt on the beginning when you first started.

Your Car is Off the Place of your Travel

It is possible to do this with your vehicle wherever you travel. Select a parking area which is located a bit further from the destination every time you park. So, you'll need to walk which will allow you to get an exercise routine in the process of getting to every destination. A walk of just 3 minutes through the parking area can increase around 20 to 30 minutes worth of walking.

A healthy diet is an essential aspect of living regardless of whether or not you're looking to lose weight or prevent diseases that could be a threat. Most people today know that there are plenty of healthy foods they can prepare at home. However, it can be a challenge to alter your routine and incorporate the right type of food in your diet. To overcome this anxiety, Kaizen can be helpful.

Conclusion

Kaizen is, as you may have read from this text, refers to a mental state that is a method, an approach, tool, a strategy an approach to culture, and a journey. Anything that needs to change to be better is based on the principles of Kaizen.

Many businesses embrace the concept to stay ahead of other companies in the market. Adopting Kaizen in the workplace is different than accepting it within your family. It is more difficult to create personal change in your own life, especially when you have to face your emotional state that you are.

It can be difficult to keep your the emotions in check. Sometimes, your emotions can make it difficult to make the right choice. It's hard to emphasize enough that it is crucial to reflect on your own values, goals and mission. These are the things to consider when making changes or taking decisions.

It's normal to retrace your steps slightly, but it's absurd to sacrifice your goals simply due to the fact that you have took a step back.

This is why it's important to develop routines that adhere to the Kaizen principle. This keeps you engaged on the field for long enough to endure the pressure of external forces.

The Kaizen concept isn't similar to making a resolution for the New Year. The former focuses on gradual changes The issue with the former is the fact that what that it promotes can be sudden and often not long-lasting. For instance, you cannot just quit drinking. If you drink frequently, you'll experience withdrawal symptoms. And even if you were able to avoid drinking for a few days, the chance of returning to the old habits is very high. This is due to the fact that your objective is not aligned with your goals effectively.

If you're at this section of the book, I am sure that you'll be able to realize your goal that is guided by Kaizen's principles. Kaizen.

Take action on what you've learned. It really does work!

My pleasure is to share important information to those in need of it. I am confident that you'll improve your mental and physical well-being and live a better quality of life by applying what you read in these pages.

Good luck and thanks for your support!

www.ingramcontent.com/pod-product-compliance
Lightning Source LLC
Chambersburg PA
CBHW050404120526
44590CB00015B/1827